Walking Meditations
Journal

Walk Into Divine Balance

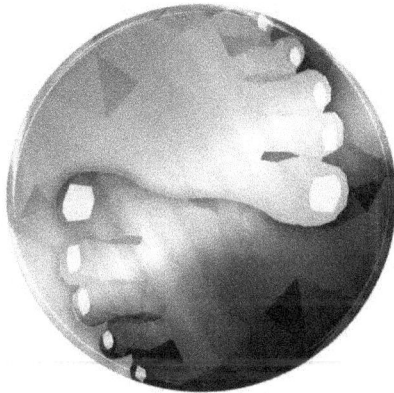

Tawan Chester Ph.D., Mhyp.D, Ppht.

Yasmin Best Ppht.

Dumouriez Publishing
Jacksonville, Florida

Walking Meditations Journal: Walk Into Divine Balance

Dumouriez Publishing
Jacksonville, Florida, USA
www.dpublishing.com

PUBLISHER'S NOTE
The information contained herein is not intended for therapy, medical, or religious purposes. The techniques are not substitutes for the treatment of a medical practitioner or professional. Use is at the reader's sole discretion and risk.

Tawan Chester Ph.D., Mhyp.D, Ppht. & Yasmin Best Ppht.

Workshop information can be obtained by visiting www.walkingmeditations.org We invite you to join us on social media outlets such as: Facebook, Instagram, Twitter, YouTube, WordPress, etc.

.

ISBN13: 978-2607-005-9

Preface

Walking Meditations incorporates aspects of meditation, labyrinths, and sacred altars to help bring about balance in your life by accessing and communicating with the Devine Essence in yourself and the world around you. You are able to understand yourself and the world around you using walking meditations.

This journal was created with you in mind and is the perfect companion to the Walking Meditations workshop. It helps to support your efforts and continued success with enhancing and balancing. The journal contains challenges (exercises) that help you hone your ability to connect with your Divine Self and the Divine Essence within others. You are also given challenges (exercises) to assist you in becoming better acquainted with your physical body, help increase your ability to manifest your desires and areas for recording your experiences.

The challenges (exercises) help to increase your comfort level and knowledge base for interacting with outside objects. Each object has a different DNA or atomic structure that results in a unique physical appearance. Many objects and species have a special method of communicating and the challenges presented in this journal help you tap into these different forms.

How to Use This Journal

The challenges are arranged to help you progress with the greatest of ease. Begin with *Part 1 Activating & Awakening*. Work through each challenge at your own pace before moving to the next one. The best results come when you take your time. During each challenge, you will be increasing your vocabulary, knowledge base, skill level and comfort level so that future challenges will enjoyable and easy.

Once you have completed the first section, move on to *Part 2 Engaging*. Start at the beginning and complete each challenge in order. Unless otherwise noted you are at liberty to browse through this section and take each challenge as it interests you. *Part 3 Walking Meditations* consists of the templates used in the workshop. These can be used at any time by following the information you received in the workshop or from the workbook. *Part 4 Manifesting* is the last of the challenges and should be approached last as it will require the increased comfort and skill level you gained from the previous sections. *Part 5, Journaling,* is an area for you to express yourself. Use this section anytime as frequently as possible.

Pictures and symbols comprise a universal language. Each species has a somewhat unique language that it uses to communicate with. Therefore, you may find that objects and animals lean more toward this type of communication. Technology and social media has taken this approach with the use of Icons and Emojis. These two groups of symbols rely on the commonalities of peoples with different languages and cultures. The vocabulary is built on your interactions with other objects. Journal in the vocabulary section any reoccurring patterns, sounds, aromas, and sensations that happen because they are the exchanges between you and objects.

Use the information gained through Walking Meditations to become more in tune with the world around you. Please do not try to pry into the personal side of others. Moving from a state of Divine Essence, you are able to see why people act or react. If used correctly the information gain can help to improve the relationships you share with others.

Key notes to remember:

- Start with the easiest challenge first

- Always move from the state of Divine Self

- Always approach an object from the Divine Self state

- Always connect and engage an object from the Divine Self state

- Move in, through, and around the object to gather information

- Always engage all of your physical senses, emotions, and intuitive sensing

- Your ethereal sensing (Clair essence), will be your greatest tool

TABLE OF CONTENTS

Part 1

Activating
&
Awakening

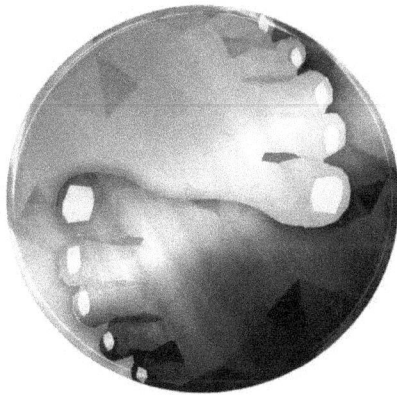

Strengthen and stabilize through meditation

Activating Hands POIs Challenge 1:

Select a POI area on the hands that corresponds with area of the body you would like to explore. Diagram the body part or write it in the space below. Massage and activate the POI using the techniques covered in the workbook and the workshop. Record information pertaining to that experience.

Diagram or list the targeted body part

Date:_____ Start Time:_____ End Time:_____

Sound(s) used: _____

Aroma(s) used: _____

POI targeted:

      Hands: _____

Type of massage:

      Fingers ____ Thumbs ____ Combination ____

Length of massage used per hand:

Activation strokes used:

   Tapping ___ Pressing ___ Circular ___ Combination ___

Expectations: _____

_____

_____

_____

Sensory information:

   Before: _____

   During: _____

   After: _____

Emotions/Feelings:

   Before: _____

   During: _____

   After: _____

Thoughts:

   Before: _____

   During: _____

   After: _____

Experience:_____

_____

_____

_____

_____

Activating Hands POIs Challenge 2:

Select a POI area on the hands that corresponds with area of the body you would like to explore. Diagram the body part or write it in the space below. Massage and activate the POI using the techniques covered in the workbook and the workshop. Record information pertaining to that experience.

```
┌─────────────────────────────────────────────────────┐
│ Diagram or list the targeted body part               │
│                                                       │
│                                                       │
│                                                       │
│                                                       │
│                                                       │
│                                                       │
│                                                       │
│                                                       │
│                                                       │
└─────────────────────────────────────────────────────┘
```

Date:_____ Start Time:_____ End Time:_____

Sound(s) used: _____

Aroma(s) used: _____

POI targeted:

      Hands: _____

Type of massage:

      Fingers ____ Thumbs ____ Combination ____

Length of massage used per hand:

Activation strokes used:

   Tapping ____ Pressing ____ Circular ____ Combination ____

Expectations: _____

_____

_____

_____

Sensory information:

   Before: _____

   During: _____

   After: _____

Emotions/Feelings:

   Before: _____

   During: _____

   After: _____

Thoughts:

   Before: _____

   During: _____

   After: _____

Experience: _____

_____

_____

_____

_____

Activating Hands POIs Challenge 3:

Select a POI area on the hands that corresponds with area of the body you would like to explore. Diagram the body part or write it in the space below. Massage and activate the POI using the techniques covered in the workbook and the workshop. Record information pertaining to that experience.

Diagram or list the targeted body part

Date:_____ Start Time:_____   End Time:_____

Sound(s) used: _____

Aroma(s) used: _____

POI targeted:

       Hands: _____

Type of massage:

       Fingers ____ Thumbs ____ Combination ____

Length of massage used per hand:

Activation strokes used:

  Tapping ＿＿ Pressing ＿＿ Circular ＿＿ Combination ＿＿

Expectations: ＿＿＿＿＿＿＿＿＿＿＿＿＿＿＿＿＿＿＿＿＿＿

＿＿＿＿＿＿＿＿＿＿＿＿＿＿＿＿＿＿＿＿＿＿＿＿＿＿＿＿

＿＿＿＿＿＿＿＿＿＿＿＿＿＿＿＿＿＿＿＿＿＿＿＿＿＿＿＿

＿＿＿＿＿＿＿＿＿＿＿＿＿＿＿＿＿＿＿＿＿＿＿＿＿＿＿＿

Sensory information:

  Before: ＿＿＿＿＿＿＿＿＿＿＿＿＿＿＿＿＿＿＿＿＿＿＿

  During: ＿＿＿＿＿＿＿＿＿＿＿＿＿＿＿＿＿＿＿＿＿＿＿

  After: ＿＿＿＿＿＿＿＿＿＿＿＿＿＿＿＿＿＿＿＿＿＿＿＿

Emotions/Feelings:

  Before: ＿＿＿＿＿＿＿＿＿＿＿＿＿＿＿＿＿＿＿＿＿＿＿

  During: ＿＿＿＿＿＿＿＿＿＿＿＿＿＿＿＿＿＿＿＿＿＿＿

  After: ＿＿＿＿＿＿＿＿＿＿＿＿＿＿＿＿＿＿＿＿＿＿＿＿

Thoughts:

  Before: ＿＿＿＿＿＿＿＿＿＿＿＿＿＿＿＿＿＿＿＿＿＿＿

  During: ＿＿＿＿＿＿＿＿＿＿＿＿＿＿＿＿＿＿＿＿＿＿＿

  After: ＿＿＿＿＿＿＿＿＿＿＿＿＿＿＿＿＿＿＿＿＿＿＿＿

Experience:＿＿＿＿＿＿＿＿＿＿＿＿＿＿＿＿＿＿＿＿＿＿＿

＿＿＿＿＿＿＿＿＿＿＿＿＿＿＿＿＿＿＿＿＿＿＿＿＿＿＿＿

＿＿＿＿＿＿＿＿＿＿＿＿＿＿＿＿＿＿＿＿＿＿＿＿＿＿＿＿

＿＿＿＿＿＿＿＿＿＿＿＿＿＿＿＿＿＿＿＿＿＿＿＿＿＿＿＿

＿＿＿＿＿＿＿＿＿＿＿＿＿＿＿＿＿＿＿＿＿＿＿＿＿＿＿＿

Activating Feet POIs Challenge 1:

Select a POI area on the feet that corresponds with area of the body you would like to explore. Diagram the body part or write it in the space below. Massage and activate the POI using the techniques covered in the workbook and the workshop. Record information pertaining to that experience.

Diagram or list the targeted body part

Date:_____ Start Time:_____ End Time:_____

Sound(s) used: _____

Aroma(s) used: _____

POI targeted:

      Feet: _____

Type of massage:

      Fingers ____ Thumbs ____ Combination ____

Length of massage used per foot:

Activation strokes used:

Tapping ____ Pressing ____ Circular ____ Combination ____

Expectations: _____

_____

_____

_____

Sensory information:

    Before: _____

    During: _____

    After: _____

Emotions/Feelings:

    Before: _____

    During: _____

    After: _____

Thoughts:

    Before: _____

    During: _____

    After: _____

Experience:_____

_____

_____

_____

_____

Activating Feet POIs Challenge 2:

Select a POI area on the feet that corresponds with area of the body you would like to explore. Diagram the body part or write it in the space below. Massage and activate the POI using the techniques covered in the workbook and the workshop. Record information pertaining to that experience.

Diagram or list the targeted body part

Date:_____ Start Time:_____   End Time:_____

Sound(s) used: _____

Aroma(s) used: _____

POI targeted:

      Feet: _____

Type of massage:

         Fingers ____ Thumbs ____ Combination ____

Length of massage used per foot:

Activation strokes used:

Tapping ____ Pressing ____ Circular ____ Combination ____

Expectations: _____

_____

_____

_____

Sensory information:

Before: _____

During: _____

After: _____

Emotions/Feelings:

Before: _____

During: _____

After: _____

Thoughts:

Before: _____

During: _____

After: _____

Experience:_____

_____

_____

_____

_____

Activating Feet POIs Challenge 3:

Select a POI area on the feet that corresponds with area of the body you would like to explore. Diagram the body part or write it in the space below. Massage and activate the POI using the techniques covered in the workbook and the workshop. Record information pertaining to that experience.

```
Diagram or list the targeted body part




```

Date:_____ Start Time:_____   End Time:_____

Sound(s) used: _____

Aroma(s) used: _____

POI targeted:

        Feet: _____

Type of massage:

        Fingers ____ Thumbs ____ Combination ____

Length of massage used per foot:

Activation strokes used:

  Tapping ____ Pressing ____ Circular ____ Combination ____

Expectations: _____

_____

_____

_____

Sensory information:

  Before: _____

  During: _____

  After: _____

Emotions/Feelings:

  Before: _____

  During: _____

  After: _____

Thoughts:

  Before: _____

  During: _____

  After: _____

Experience:_____

_____

_____

_____

_____

Awakening Divine-Self Challenge 1

Sit comfortably in an area where you will not be disturbed. Following the techniques learned in the workshop and the steps in the Walking Meditations workbook awaken the Divine-Self. In this challenge your goal is to consciously feel, sense, and observe the presence of your Divine-Self. Record information pertaining to that experience.

Date:_____   Start Time:_____   End Time:_____

Sound(s) used: _____

Aroma(s) used: _____

POI targeted:

      Hands/feet: _____

Type of massage:

         Fingers ____ Thumbs ____ Combination ____

Length of massage used per hand/feet:

Activation strokes used:

      Tapping ____ Pressing ____ Circular ____ Combination ____

Expectations: _____

_____

_____

Sensory information:

    Before: _____

    During: _____

    After: _____

Body Sensations:

    Before: _____

    During: _____

    After: _____

Emotions/Feelings:

    Before: _____

    During: _____

    After: _____

Thoughts/Reactions:

    Before: _____

    During: _____

    After: _____

Experience: _____

_____

_____

_____

_____

_____

Sit comfortably in an area where you will not be disturbed. Following the techniques learned in the workshop and the steps in the Walking Meditations workbook awaken the Divine-Self. In this challenge your goal is to consciously feel, sense, and observe the presence of your Divine-Self. Record information pertaining to that experience.

Date:_____ Start Time:_____ End Time:_____

Sound(s) used: _____

Aroma(s) used: _____

POI targeted:

      Hands/feet: _____

Type of massage:

      Fingers ____ Thumbs ____ Combination ____

Length of massage used per hand/feet:

Activation strokes used:

      Tapping ____ Pressing ____ Circular ____ Combination ____

Expectations: _____
_____
_____

Sensory information:

     Before: _____

     During: _____

     After: _____

Body Sensations:

     Before: _____

     During: _____

     After: _____

Emotions/Feelings:

     Before: _____

     During: _____

     After: _____

Thoughts/Reactions:

     Before: _____

     During: _____

     After: _____

Experience: _____

_____

_____

_____

_____

_____

Sit comfortably in an area where you will not be disturbed. Following the techniques learned in the workshop and the steps in the Walking Meditations workbook awaken the Divine-Self. In this challenge your goal is to consciously feel, sense, and observe the presence of your Divine-Self. Record information pertaining to that experience.

Date:_____   Start Time:_____   End Time:_____

Sound(s) used: _____

Aroma(s) used: _____

POI targeted:

       Hands/feet: _____

Type of massage:

              Fingers ____ Thumbs ____ Combination ____

Length of massage used per hand/feet:

Activation strokes used:

       Tapping ____ Pressing ____ Circular ____ Combination ____

Expectations: _____

_____

_____

Sensory information:

      Before: _____

      During: _____

      After: _____

Body Sensations:

      Before: _____

      During: _____

      After: _____

Emotions/Feelings:

      Before: _____

      During: _____

      After: _____

Thoughts/Reactions:

      Before: _____

      During: _____

      After: _____

Experience: _____

_____

_____

_____

_____

_____

Expanding Divine Self Challenge 1a*

Sit comfortably in an area where you will not be disturbed. Following the techniques learned in the workshop and the steps in the Walking Meditations workbook expand your Divine Self. In this challenge your goal is to consciously expand your Divine-Essence outward in a specific direction. Record information pertaining to that experience. *Complete the Awaken Divine Self challenge before doing this one.

Date:_____   Start Time:_____   End Time:_____

Sound(s) used: _____

Aroma(s) used: _____

POI targeted:

      Hands/feet: _____

Expand outward:

      One direction _____ Two directions _____

Type of massage:

      Fingers ____ Thumbs ____ Combination ____

Length of massage used per hand/feet:

Activation strokes used:

      Tapping ____ Pressing ____ Circular ____ Combination ____

Expectations: _____

_____

Sensory information: _____

_____

Body Sensations: _____

_____

Emotions/Feelings: _____

_____

Thoughts/Reactions: _____

_____

Temperature fluctuations:_____

_____

Illustrate or describe the activity or movement within the Divine-Essence:

Experience: _____

_____

_____

_____

_____

Expanding Divine Self Challenge 2a*

Sit comfortably in an area where you will not be disturbed. Following the techniques learned in the workshop and the steps in the Walking Meditations workbook expand your Divine Self. In this challenge your goal is to consciously expand your Divine-Essence outward in a specific direction. Record information pertaining to that experience. *Complete the Awaken Divine Self challenge before doing this one.

Date:_____   Start Time:_____   End Time:_____

Sound(s) used: _____

Aroma(s) used: _____

POI targeted:

      Hands/feet: _____

Expand outward:

      One direction _____ Two directions _____

Type of massage:

      Fingers ____ Thumbs ____ Combination ____

Length of massage used per hand/feet:

Activation strokes used:

      Tapping ____ Pressing ____ Circular ____ Combination ____

Expectations: _____

Sensory information: _____

Body Sensations: _____

Emotions/Feelings: _____

Thoughts/Reactions: _____

Temperature fluctuations:_____

Illustrate or describe the activity or movement within the Divine-Essence:

Experience: _____

_____

_____

_____

_____

Expanding Divine Self Challenge 3a*

Sit comfortably in an area where you will not be disturbed. Following the techniques learned in the workshop and the steps in the Walking Meditations workbook expand your Divine Self. In this challenge your goal is to consciously expand your Divine-Essence outward in a specific direction. Record information pertaining to that experience. *Complete the Awaken Divine Self challenge before doing this one.

Date:_____   Start Time:_____   End Time:_____

Sound(s) used: _____

Aroma(s) used: _____

POI targeted:

      Hands/feet: _____

Expand outward:

      One direction _____ Two directions _____

Type of massage:

      Fingers ___ Thumbs ___ Combination ___

Length of massage used per hand/feet:

Activation strokes used:

      Tapping ___ Pressing ___ Circular ___ Combination ___

Expectations: _____

_____

Sensory information: _____

_____

Body Sensations: _____

_____

Emotions/Feelings: _____

_____

Thoughts/Reactions: _____

_____

Temperature fluctuations:_____

_____

Illustrate or describe the activity or movement within the Divine-Essence:

Experience: _____

_____

_____

_____

_____

Expanding Divine Self Challenge 1b*

Sit comfortably in an area where you will not be disturbed. Following the techniques learned in the workshop and the steps in the Walking Meditations workbook expand your Divine Self. In this challenge your goal is to consciously expand your Divine-Essence outward multidirectionally to a specified distance. Record that experience. *Complete the Expanding Divine Self challenges 'A'.

Date:_____ Start Time:_____ End Time:_____

Sound(s) used: _____

Aroma(s) used: _____

POI targeted:

     Hands/feet: _____

Expand outward:

     3 Feet _____ 5 Feet _____ 10 Feet _____ 15 Feet _____

Type of massage:

     Fingers ____ Thumbs ____ Combination ____

Length of massage used per hand/feet:

Activation strokes used:

     Tapping ____ Pressing ____ Circular ____ Combination ____

Expectations: _____

_____

Sensory information: _____

_____

Body Sensations: _____

_____

Emotions/Feelings: _____

_____

Thoughts/Reactions: _____

_____

Temperature fluctuations:_____

_____

Illustrate or describe the activity or movement within the Divine-Essence:

Experience: _____

_____

_____

_____

_____

Expanding Divine Self Challenge 2b*

Sit comfortably in an area where you will not be disturbed. Following the techniques learned in the workshop and the steps in the Walking Meditations workbook expand your Divine Self. In this challenge your goal is to consciously expand your Divine-Essence outward multidirectionally to a specified distance. Record that experience. *Complete the Expanding Divine Self challenges 'A'.

Date:_____   Start Time:_____   End Time:_____

Sound(s) used: _____

Aroma(s) used: _____

POI targeted:

      Hands/feet: _____

Expand outward:

      3 Feet _____ 5 Feet _____ 10 Feet _____ 15 Feet _____

Type of massage:

      Fingers ___ Thumbs ___ Combination ___

Length of massage used per hand/feet:

Activation strokes used:

      Tapping ___ Pressing ___ Circular ___ Combination ___

Expectations: _____

_____

Sensory information: _____

_____

Body Sensations: _____

_____

Emotions/Feelings: _____

_____

Thoughts/Reactions: _____

_____

Temperature fluctuations:_____

_____

Illustrate or describe the activity or movement within the Divine-Essence:

Experience: _____

_____

_____

_____

_____

Expanding Divine Self Challenge 3b*

Sit comfortably in an area where you will not be disturbed. Following the techniques learned in the workshop and the steps in the Walking Meditations workbook expand your Divine Self. In this challenge your goal is to consciously expand your Divine-Essence outward multidirectionally to a specified distance. Record that experience. *Complete the Expanding Divine Self challenges 'A'.

Date:_____   Start Time:_____   End Time:_____

Sound(s) used: _____

Aroma(s) used: _____

POI targeted:

     Hands/feet: _____

Expand outward:

     3 Feet _____ 5 Feet _____ 10 Feet _____ 15 Feet _____

Type of massage:

     Fingers ___ Thumbs ___ Combination ___

Length of massage used per hand/feet:

Activation strokes used:

     Tapping ___ Pressing ___ Circular ___ Combination ___

Expectations: _____

_____

Sensory information: _____

_____

Body Sensations: _____

_____

Emotions/Feelings: _____

_____

Thoughts/Reactions: _____

_____

Temperature fluctuations:_____

_____

Illustrate or describe the activity or movement within the Divine-Essence:

Experience: _____

_____

_____

_____

_____

Divine Connections Challenge 1

Sit comfortably in an area where you will not be disturbed. Following the techniques learned in the workshop and the steps in the Walking Meditations workbook for Divine Connections. In this challenge your goal is to consciously allow your Divine-Essence to connect with the Divine Essence of another. outward to meet and greet the Divine-Essence of an object (please do not communicate or engage the object by trying to exchange information. Record information pertaining to that experience.

Date:_____ Start Time:_____ End Time:_____

Sound(s) used: _____

Aroma(s) used:_____

POI targeted:

     Hands/feet: _____

Type of massage:

     Fingers ____ Thumbs ____ Combination ____

Length of massage used per hand/feet:

Activation strokes used:

     Tapping ____ Pressing ____ Circular ____ Combination ____

Physical distance from object: _____

Expectations: _____

_____

_____

Greeting used: _____

_____

Describe the initial meeting (awkward, exciting, nervous, strained, relaxed, etc):

Overall sentiment of the connection:

Body Sensations: _____

_____

Emotions/Feelings: _____

_____

Thoughts/Reactions: _____

_____

Illustrate or describe the activity or movement within your Divine-Essence:

Illustrate or describe the activity or movement within the object's Divine-Essence:

Experience:_____

_____

_____

Divine Connections Challenge 2

Sit comfortably in an area where you will not be disturbed. Following the techniques learned in the workshop and the steps in the Walking Meditations workbook for Divine Connections. In this challenge your goal is to consciously allow your Divine-Essence to connect with the Divine Essence of another. outward to meet and greet the Divine-Essence of an object (please do not communicate or engage the object by trying to exchange information. Record information pertaining to that experience.

Date:_____   Start Time:_____   End Time:_____

Sound(s) used: _____

Aroma(s) used:_____

POI targeted:

       Hands/feet: _____

Type of massage:

       Fingers ____ Thumbs ____ Combination ____

Length of massage used per hand/feet:

Activation strokes used:

       Tapping ____ Pressing ____ Circular ____ Combination ____

Physical distance from object: _____

Expectations: _____

_____

_____

Greeting used: _____

_____

Describe the initial meeting (awkward, exciting, nervous, strained, relaxed, etc):

Overall sentiment of the connection:

Body Sensations: _____

_____

Emotions/Feelings: _____

_____

Thoughts/Reactions: _____

_____

Illustrate or describe the activity or movement within your Divine-Essence:

Illustrate or describe the activity or movement within the object's Divine-Essence:

Experience:_____

_____

_____

Divine Connections Challenge 3

Sit comfortably in an area where you will not be disturbed. Following the techniques learned in the workshop and the steps in the Walking Meditations workbook for Divine Connections. In this challenge your goal is to consciously allow your Divine-Essence to connect with the Divine Essence of another. outward to meet and greet the Divine-Essence of an object (please do not communicate or engage the object by trying to exchange information. Record information pertaining to that experience.

Date:_____ Start Time:_____ End Time:_____

Sound(s) used: _____

Aroma(s) used:_____

POI targeted:

      Hands/feet: _____

Type of massage:

          Fingers ___ Thumbs ___ Combination ___

Length of massage used per hand/feet:

Activation strokes used:

      Tapping ___ Pressing ___ Circular ___ Combination ___

Physical distance from object: _____

Expectations: _____

_____

_____

Greeting used: _____

_____

Describe the initial meeting (awkward, exciting, nervous, strained, relaxed, etc):

Overall sentiment of the connection:

Body Sensations: _____

_____

Emotions/Feelings: _____

_____

Thoughts/Reactions: _____

_____

Illustrate or describe the activity or movement within your Divine-Essence:

Illustrate or describe the activity or movement within the object's Divine-Essence:

Experience:_____

_____

_____

Part 2

Engaging

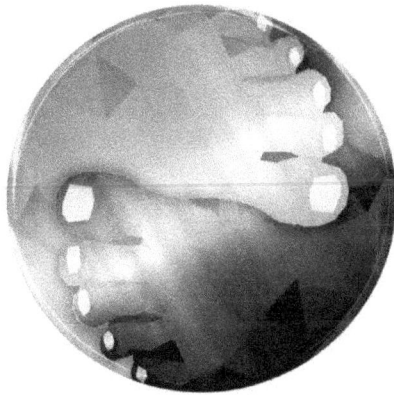

Live in your state of Divine balance with meditation

Object Challenge 1:

Select an object in the area or space that you are occupying. Diagram the object in the space below. Connect and engage with the object through the Divine-Self aspect using the information and techniques from the workbook and workshop. Record information pertaining to that experience.

```
Diagram the object in the Walking Meditations' path containing the object




```

Date:_____   Start Time:_____   End Time:_____

Sound(s) used: _____

Aroma(s) used:_____

POI targeted:

      Hands:_____

      Feet: _____

Expectations: _____

_____

_____

Sensory information (usually from object):

    Before: _____

    During: _____

    After: _____

Emotions/Feelings (from the object/yourself):

    Before: _____

    During: _____

    After: _____

Thoughts: (usually from you)

    Before: _____

    During: _____

    After: _____

Words/Statements (from the object/yourself):

    Before: _____

    During: _____

    After: _____

Attributes & characteristics experience: _____

_____

Surface/Texture: _____

Composition: _____

Temperature: _____

Density: _____

Movement: _____

Location/place: _____

Object Challenge 2:

Select an object in the area or space that you are occupying. Diagram the object in the space below. Connect and engage with the object through the Divine-Self aspect using the information and techniques from the workbook and workshop. Record information pertaining to that experience.

> Diagram the object in the Walking Meditations' path containing the object

Date:_____   Start Time:_____   End Time:_____

Sound(s) used: _____

Aroma(s) used:_____

POI targeted:

      Hands:_____

      Feet: _____

Expectations: _____

_____

_____

Sensory information (usually from object):

    Before: _____

    During: _____

    After: _____

Emotions/Feelings (from the object/yourself):

    Before: _____

    During: _____

    After: _____

Thoughts: (usually from you)

    Before: _____

    During: _____

    After: _____

Words/Statements (from the object/yourself):

    Before: _____

    During: _____

    After: _____

Attributes & characteristics experience: _____

_____

Surface/Texture: _____

Composition: _____

Temperature: _____

Density: _____

Movement: _____

Location/place: _____

Object Challenge 3:

Select an object in the area or space that you are occupying. Diagram the object in the space below. Connect and engage with the object through the Divine-Self aspect using the information and techniques from the workbook and workshop. Record information pertaining to that experience.

Diagram the object in the Walking Meditations' path containing the object

---

Date:_____ Start Time:_____ End Time:_____

Sound(s) used: _____

Aroma(s) used:_____

POI targeted:

      Hands:_____

      Feet: _____

Expectations: _____

_____

_____

Sensory information (usually from object):

     Before: _____

     During: _____

     After: _____

Emotions/Feelings (from the object/yourself):

     Before: _____

     During: _____

     After: _____

Thoughts: (usually from you)

     Before: _____

     During: _____

     After: _____

Words/Statements (from the object/yourself):

     Before: _____

     During: _____

     After: _____

Attributes & characteristics experience: _____

_____

Surface/Texture: _____

Composition: _____

Temperature: _____

Density: _____

Movement: _____

Location/place: _____

Fire Object Challenge 1:

Select an object made of fire or containing mostly fire. Diagram the object in the space below. Connect and engage with the object through the Divine-Self aspect using the information and techniques from the workbook and workshop. Record the experience.

Diagram the object in the Walking Meditations' path containing the object

Date:_____   Start Time:_____   End Time:_____

Sound(s) used: _____

Aroma(s) used: _____

POI targeted:

      Hands:_____

      Feet: _____

Expectations: _____

_____

_____

Sensory information (usually from object):

        Before: _____

        During: _____

        After: _____

Emotions/Feelings (from the object/yourself):

        Before:_____

        During: _____

        After: _____

Thoughts: (usually from you)

        Before: _____

        During: _____

        After: _____

Words/Statements (from the object/yourself):

        Before:_____

        During: _____

        After: _____

Attributes & characteristics experience: _____

_____

Composition: _____

Temperature: _____

Movement: _____

Interaction:_ _____

Temperament: _____

Connection: _____

Nature: _____

Fire Object Challenge 2:

Select an object made of fire or containing mostly fire. Diagram the object in the space below. Connect and engage with the object through the Divine-Self aspect using the information and techniques from the workbook and workshop. Record the experience.

Diagram the object in the Walking Meditations' path containing the object

Date:_____ Start Time:_____ End Time:_____

Sound(s) used: _____

Aroma(s) used: _____

POI targeted:

      Hands:_____

      Feet: _____

Expectations: _____

_____

_____

Sensory information (usually from object):

    Before: _____

    During: _____

    After: _____

Emotions/Feelings (from the object/yourself):

    Before:_____

    During: _____

    After: _____

Thoughts: (usually from you)

    Before: _____

    During: _____

    After: _____

Words/Statements (from the object/yourself):

    Before:_____

    During: _____

    After: _____

Attributes & characteristics experience: _____

_____

Composition: _____

Temperature: _____

Movement: _____

Interaction:_ _____

Temperament: _____

Connection: _____

Nature: _____

Fire Object Challenge 3:

Select an object made of fire or containing mostly fire. Diagram the object in the space below. Connect and engage with the object through the Divine-Self aspect using the information and techniques from the workbook and workshop. Record the experience.

> Diagram the object in the Walking Meditations' path containing the object

Date:_____   Start Time:_____   End Time:_____

Sound(s) used: _____

Aroma(s) used: _____

POI targeted:

    Hands:_____

    Feet: _____

Expectations: _____

_____

_____

Sensory information (usually from object):

    Before: _____

    During: _____

    After: _____

Emotions/Feelings (from the object/yourself):

    Before:_____

    During: _____

    After: _____

Thoughts: (usually from you)

    Before: _____

    During: _____

    After: _____

Words/Statements (from the object/yourself):

    Before:_____

    During: _____

    After: _____

Attributes & characteristics experience: _____

_____

Composition: _____

Temperature: _____

Movement: _____

Interaction:_ _____

Temperament: _____

Connection: _____

Nature: _____

Liquid Object Challenge 1:

Select a liquid object that is not ethereal. Diagram the object in the space below. Connect and engage with the object through the Divine-Self aspect using the information and techniques from the workbook and workshop. Record information pertaining to that experience.

Diagram the object in the Walking Meditations' path containing the object

Date:_____ Start Time:_____ End Time:_____

Sound(s) used: _____

Aroma(s) used: _____

POI targeted:

　　　　Hands: _____

　　　　Feet:_____

Expectations: _____

_____

Sensory information (usually from object):

    Before: _____

    During:_____

    After: _____

Emotions/Feelings (from the object/yourself):

    Before: _____

    During: _____

    After: _____

Thoughts: (usually from you)

    Before: _____

    During: _____

    After: _____

Words/Statements (from the object/yourself):

    Before: _____

    During: _____

    After: _____

Attributes & characteristics experience: _____

_____

Composition: _____

Temperature: _____

Density: _____

Movement: _____

Location/place: _____

Liquid Object Challenge 2:

Select a liquid object that is not ethereal. Diagram the object in the space below. Connect and engage with the object through the Divine-Self aspect using the information and techniques from the workbook and workshop. Record information pertaining to that experience.

Diagram the object in the Walking Meditations' path containing the object

---

Date:_____   Start Time:_____   End Time:_____

Sound(s) used: _____

Aroma(s) used: _____

POI targeted:

      Hands: _____

      Feet:_____

Expectations: _____

_____

Sensory information (usually from object):

    Before: _____

    During:_____

    After: _____

Emotions/Feelings (from the object/yourself):

    Before: _____

    During: _____

    After: _____

Thoughts: (usually from you)

    Before: _____

    During: _____

    After: _____

Words/Statements (from the object/yourself):

    Before: _____

    During: _____

    After: _____

Attributes & characteristics experience: _____

_____

Composition: _____

Temperature: _____

Density: _____

Movement: _____

Location/place: _____

Liquid Object Challenge 3:

Select a liquid object that is not ethereal. Diagram the object in the space below. Connect and engage with the object through the Divine-Self aspect using the information and techniques from the workbook and workshop. Record information pertaining to that experience.

Diagram the object in the Walking Meditations' path containing the object

---

Date:_____   Start Time:_____   End Time:_____

Sound(s) used: _____

Aroma(s) used: _____

POI targeted:

      Hands: _____

      Feet:_____

Expectations: _____

_____

Sensory information (usually from object):

Before: _____

During: _____

After: _____

Emotions/Feelings (from the object/yourself):

Before: _____

During: _____

After: _____

Thoughts: (usually from you)

Before: _____

During: _____

After: _____

Words/Statements (from the object/yourself):

Before: _____

During: _____

After: _____

Attributes & characteristics experience: _____

_____

Composition: _____

Temperature: _____

Density: _____

Movement: _____

Location/place: _____

Metal Object Challenge 1:

Select a metal object that is not ethereal. Diagram the object in the space below. Connect and engage with the object through the Divine-Self aspect using the information and techniques from the workbook and workshop. Record information pertaining to that experience.

Diagram the object in the Walking Meditations' path containing the object

Date:_____ Start Time:_____ End Time:_____

Sound(s) used: _____

Aroma(s) used: _____

POI targeted:

Hands:_____

Feet: _____

Expectations: _____

_____

Sensory information (usually from object):

    Before: _____

    During: _____

    After: _____

Emotions/Feelings (from the object/yourself):

    Before:_____

    During: _____

    After: _____

Thoughts: (usually from you)

    Before: _____

    During: _____

    After: _____

Words/Statements (from the object/yourself):

    Before: _____

    During: _____

    After: _____

Attributes & characteristics experience: _____

_____

Surface/Texture: _____

Composition: _____

Temperature: _____

Density: _____

Movement: _____

Location/place: _____

Metal Object Challenge 2:

Select a metal object that is not ethereal. Diagram the object in the space below. Connect and engage with the object through the Divine-Self aspect using the information and techniques from the workbook and workshop. Record information pertaining to that experience.

> Diagram the object in the Walking Meditations' path containing the object

Date:_____ Start Time:_____ End Time:_____

Sound(s) used: _____

Aroma(s) used: _____

POI targeted:

      Hands:_____

      Feet: _____

Expectations: _____

_____

Sensory information (usually from object):

    Before: _____

    During: _____

    After: _____

Emotions/Feelings (from the object/yourself):

    Before:_____

    During: _____

    After: _____

Thoughts: (usually from you)

    Before: _____

    During: _____

    After: _____

Words/Statements (from the object/yourself):

    Before: _____

    During: _____

    After: _____

Attributes & characteristics experience: _____

_____

Surface/Texture: _____

Composition: _____

Temperature: _____

Density: _____

Movement: _____

Location/place: _____

Metal Object Challenge 3:

Select a metal object that is not ethereal. Diagram the object in the space below. Connect and engage with the object through the Divine-Self aspect using the information and techniques from the workbook and workshop. Record information pertaining to that experience.

Diagram the object in the Walking Meditations' path containing the object

Date:_____ Start Time:_____ End Time:_____

Sound(s) used: _____

Aroma(s) used: _____

POI targeted:

      Hands:_____

      Feet: _____

Expectations: _____

_____

Sensory information (usually from object):

      Before: _____

      During: _____

      After: _____

Emotions/Feelings (from the object/yourself):

      Before:_____

      During: _____

      After: _____

Thoughts: (usually from you)

      Before: _____

      During: _____

      After: _____

Words/Statements (from the object/yourself):

      Before: _____

      During: _____

      After: _____

Attributes & characteristics experience: _____

_____

Surface/Texture: _____

Composition: _____

Temperature: _____

Density: _____

Movement: _____

Location/place: _____

Mineral Object Challenge 1:

Select a natural mineral object such as a quartz crystal or granite that is not ethereal. Diagram the object in the space below. Connect and engage with the object through the Divine-Self aspect using the information and techniques from the workbook and workshop. Record information pertaining to that experience.

Diagram the object in the Walking Meditations' path containing the object

---

Date:_____   Start Time:_____   End Time:_____

Sound(s) used: _____

Aroma(s) used: _____

POI targeted:

       Hands:_____

       Feet: _____

Expectations: _____

_____

Sensory information (usually from object):

    Before: _____

    During: _____

    After: _____

Emotions/Feelings (from the object/yourself):

    Before:_____

    During: _____

    After: _____

Thoughts: (usually from you)

    Before: _____

    During: _____

    After: _____

Words/Statements (from the object/yourself):

    Before: _____

    During: _____

    After: _____

Attributes & characteristics experience: _____

_____

Surface/Texture: _____

Composition: _____

Temperature: _____

Density: _____

Movement: _____

Location/place: _____

Mineral Object Challenge 2:

Select a natural mineral object such as a quartz crystal or granite that is not ethereal. Diagram the object in the space below. Connect and engage with the object through the Divine-Self aspect using the information and techniques from the workbook and workshop. Record information pertaining to that experience.

Diagram the object in the Walking Meditations' path containing the object

---

Date:_____ Start Time:_____ End Time:_____

Sound(s) used: _____

Aroma(s) used: _____

POI targeted:

      Hands:_____

      Feet: _____

Expectations: _____

_____

Sensory information (usually from object):

      Before: _____

      During: _____

      After: _____

Emotions/Feelings (from the object/yourself):

      Before:_____

      During: _____

      After: _____

Thoughts: (usually from you)

      Before: _____

      During: _____

      After: _____

Words/Statements (from the object/yourself):

      Before: _____

      During: _____

      After: _____

Attributes & characteristics experience: _____

_____

Surface/Texture: _____

Composition: _____

Temperature: _____

Density: _____

Movement: _____

Location/place: _____

Mineral Object Challenge 3:

Select a natural mineral object such as a quartz crystal or granite that is not ethereal. Diagram the object in the space below. Connect and engage with the object through the Divine-Self aspect using the information and techniques from the workbook and workshop. Record information pertaining to that experience.

Diagram the object in the Walking Meditations' path containing the object

Date:_____   Start Time:_____   End Time:_____

Sound(s) used: _____

Aroma(s) used: _____

POI targeted:

        Hands:_____

        Feet: _____

Expectations: _____

_____

Sensory information (usually from object):

    Before: _____

    During: _____

    After: _____

Emotions/Feelings (from the object/yourself):

    Before:_____

    During: _____

    After: _____

Thoughts: (usually from you)

    Before: _____

    During: _____

    After: _____

Words/Statements (from the object/yourself):

    Before: _____

    During: _____

    After: _____

Attributes & characteristics experience: _____

_____

Surface/Texture: _____

Composition: _____

Temperature: _____

Density: _____

Movement: _____

Location/place: _____

Smooth Object Challenge 1:

Select a smooth object that is not ethereal. Diagram the object in the space below. Connect and engage with the object through the Divine-Self aspect using the information and techniques from the workbook and workshop. Record information pertaining to that experience.

Diagram the object in the Walking Meditations' path containing the object

Date:_____ Start Time:_____ End Time:_____

Sound(s) used: _____

Aroma(s) used: _____

POI targeted:

    Hands: _____

    Feet: _____

Expectations: _____

_____

Sensory information (usually from object):

    Before: _____

    During: _____

    After: _____

Emotions/Feelings (from the object/yourself):

    Before:_____

    During: _____

    After: _____

Thoughts: (usually from you)

    Before: _____

    During: _____

    After: _____

Words/Statements (from the object/yourself):

    Before: _____

    During: _____

    After: _____

Attributes & characteristics experience: _____

_____

Surface/Texture: _____

Composition: _____

Temperature: _____

Density: _____

Movement: _____

Location/place: _____

Smooth Object Challenge 2:

Select a smooth object that is not ethereal. Diagram the object in the space below. Connect and engage with the object through the Divine-Self aspect using the information and techniques from the workbook and workshop. Record information pertaining to that experience.

Diagram the object in the Walking Meditations' path containing the object

---

Date:_____   Start Time:_____   End Time:_____

Sound(s) used: _____

Aroma(s) used: _____

POI targeted:

      Hands: _____

      Feet: _____

Expectations: _____

_____

Sensory information (usually from object):

    Before: _____

    During: _____

    After: _____

Emotions/Feelings (from the object/yourself):

    Before:_____

    During: _____

    After: _____

Thoughts: (usually from you)

    Before: _____

    During: _____

    After: _____

Words/Statements (from the object/yourself):

    Before: _____

    During: _____

    After: _____

Attributes & characteristics experience: _____

_____

Surface/Texture: _____

Composition: _____

Temperature: _____

Density: _____

Movement: _____

Location/place: _____

Smooth Object Challenge 3:

Select a smooth object that is not ethereal. Diagram the object in the space below. Connect and engage with the object through the Divine-Self aspect using the information and techniques from the workbook and workshop. Record information pertaining to that experience.

Diagram the object in the Walking Meditations' path containing the object

Date:_____   Start Time:_____   End Time:_____

Sound(s) used: _____

Aroma(s) used: _____

POI targeted:

      Hands: _____

      Feet: _____

Expectations: _____

Sensory information (usually from object):

     Before: _____

     During: _____

     After: _____

Emotions/Feelings (from the object/yourself):

     Before:_____

     During: _____

     After: _____

Thoughts: (usually from you)

     Before: _____

     During: _____

     After: _____

Words/Statements (from the object/yourself):

     Before: _____

     During: _____

     After: _____

Attributes & characteristics experience: _____

_____

Surface/Texture: _____

Composition: _____

Temperature: _____

Density: _____

Movement: _____

Location/place: _____

Textured Object Challenge 1:

Select a textured object that is not ethereal. Diagram the object in the space below. Connect and engage with the object through the Divine-Self aspect using the information and techniques from the workbook and workshop. Record information pertaining to that experience.

Diagram the object in the Walking Meditations' path containing the object

Date:_____ Start Time:_____ End Time:_____

Sound(s) used: _____

Aroma(s) used: _____

POI targeted:

Hands: _____

Feet: _____

Expectations: _____

_____

Sensory information (usually from object):

    Before: _____

    During: _____

    After: _____

Emotions/Feelings (from the object/yourself):

    Before: _____

    During: _____

    After: _____

Thoughts: (usually from you)

    Before: _____

    During: _____

    After: _____

Words/Statements (from the object/yourself):

    Before: _____

    During: _____

    After: _____

Attributes & characteristics experience: _____

_____

Surface/Texture: _____

Composition: _____

Temperature: _____

Density: _____

Movement: _____

Location/place: _____

Textured Object Challenge 2:

Select a textured object that is not ethereal. Diagram the object in the space below. Connect and engage with the object through the Divine-Self aspect using the information and techniques from the workbook and workshop. Record information pertaining to that experience.

Diagram the object in the Walking Meditations' path containing the object

Date:_____   Start Time:_____   End Time:_____

Sound(s) used: _____

Aroma(s) used: _____

POI targeted:

       Hands: _____

       Feet: _____

Expectations: _____

_____

Sensory information (usually from object):

    Before: _____

    During: _____

    After: _____

Emotions/Feelings (from the object/yourself):

    Before: _____

    During: _____

    After: _____

Thoughts: (usually from you)

    Before: _____

    During: _____

    After: _____

Words/Statements (from the object/yourself):

    Before: _____

    During: _____

    After: _____

Attributes & characteristics experience: _____

_____

Surface/Texture: _____

Composition: _____

Temperature: _____

Density: _____

Movement: _____

Location/place: _____

Textured Object Challenge 3:

Select a textured object that is not ethereal. Diagram the object in the space below. Connect and engage with the object through the Divine-Self aspect using the information and techniques from the workbook and workshop. Record information pertaining to that experience.

Diagram the object in the Walking Meditations' path containing the object

---

Date:_____   Start Time:_____   End Time:_____

Sound(s) used: _____

Aroma(s) used: _____

POI targeted:

      Hands: _____

      Feet: _____

Expectations: _____

_____

Sensory information (usually from object):

    Before: _____

    During: _____

    After: _____

Emotions/Feelings (from the object/yourself):

    Before: _____

    During: _____

    After: _____

Thoughts: (usually from you)

    Before: _____

    During: _____

    After: _____

Words/Statements (from the object/yourself):

    Before: _____

    During: _____

    After: _____

Attributes & characteristics experience: _____

_____

Surface/Texture: _____

Composition: _____

Temperature: _____

Density: _____

Movement: _____

Location/place: _____

Wood Object Challenge 1:

Select a wood object that is not ethereal. Diagram the object in the space below. Connect and engage with the object through the Divine-Self aspect using the information and techniques from the workbook and workshop. Record information pertaining to that experience.

Diagram the object in the Walking Meditations' path containing the object

Date:_____   Start Time:_____   End Time:_____

Sound(s) used: _____

Aroma(s) used: _____

POI targeted:

        Hands :_____

        Feet: _____

Expectations: _____

_____

Sensory information (usually from object):

     Before: _____

     During: _____

     After: _____

Emotions/Feelings (from the object/yourself):

     Before: _____

     During: _____

     After: _____

Thoughts: (usually from you)

     Before: _____

     During: _____

     After: _____

Words/Statements (from the object/yourself):

     Before: _____

     During: _____

     After: _____

Attributes & characteristics experience: _____

_____

Surface/Texture: _____

Composition: _____

Temperature: _____

Density: _____

Movement: _____

Location/place: _____

Wood Object Challenge 2:

Select a wood object that is not ethereal. Diagram the object in the space below. Connect and engage with the object through the Divine-Self aspect using the information and techniques from the workbook and workshop. Record information pertaining to that experience.

Diagram the object in the Walking Meditations' path containing the object

Date:_____ Start Time:_____ End Time:_____

Sound(s) used: _____

Aroma(s) used: _____

POI targeted:

      Hands :_____

      Feet: _____

Expectations: _____

_____

Sensory information (usually from object):

  Before: _____

  During: _____

  After: _____

Emotions/Feelings (from the object/yourself):

  Before: _____

  During: _____

  After: _____

Thoughts: (usually from you)

  Before: _____

  During: _____

  After: _____

Words/Statements (from the object/yourself):

  Before: _____

  During: _____

  After: _____

Attributes & characteristics experience: _____

_____

Surface/Texture: _____

Composition: _____

Temperature: _____

Density: _____

Movement: _____

Location/place: _____

Wood Object Challenge 3:

Select a wood object that is not ethereal. Diagram the object in the space below. Connect and engage with the object through the Divine-Self aspect using the information and techniques from the workbook and workshop. Record information pertaining to that experience.

Diagram the object in the Walking Meditations' path containing the object

Date:_____   Start Time:_____   End Time:_____

Sound(s) used: _____

Aroma(s) used: _____

POI targeted:

      Hands :_____

      Feet: _____

Expectations: _____

_____

Sensory information (usually from object):

    Before: _____

    During: _____

    After: _____

Emotions/Feelings (from the object/yourself):

    Before: _____

    During: _____

    After: _____

Thoughts: (usually from you)

    Before: _____

    During: _____

    After: _____

Words/Statements (from the object/yourself):

    Before: _____

    During: _____

    After: _____

Attributes & characteristics experience: _____

_____

Surface/Texture: _____

Composition: _____

Temperature: _____

Density: _____

Movement: _____

Location/place: _____

Live Plant Object Challenge 1:

Select a live plant object that is not ethereal. Diagram the object in the space below. Connect and engage with the object through the Divine-Self aspect using the information and techniques from the workbook and workshop. Record information pertaining to that experience.

Diagram the object in the Walking Meditations' path containing the object

---

Date:_____   Start Time:_____   End Time:_____

Sound(s) used: _____

Aroma(s) used: _____

POI targeted:

      Hands:_____

      Feet: _____

Expectations: _____

_____

Sensory information (usually from object):

    Before: _____

    During: _____

    After: _____

Emotions/Feelings (from the object/yourself):

    Before: _____

    During: _____

    After: _____

Thoughts: (usually from you)

    Before: _____

    During: _____

    After: _____

Words/Statements (from the object/yourself):

    Before: _____

    During: _____

    After: _____

Attributes & characteristics experience: _____

_____

Surface/Texture: _____

Composition: _____

Temperature: _____

Density: _____

Movement: _____

Location/place: _____

Live Plant Object Challenge 2:

Select a live plant object that is not ethereal. Diagram the object in the space below. Connect and engage with the object through the Divine-Self aspect using the information and techniques from the workbook and workshop. Record information pertaining to that experience.

Diagram the object in the Walking Meditations' path containing the object

Date:_____ Start Time:_____ End Time:_____

Sound(s) used: _____

Aroma(s) used: _____

POI targeted:

      Hands:_____

      Feet: _____

Expectations: _____

_____

Sensory information (usually from object):

     Before: _____

     During: _____

     After: _____

Emotions/Feelings (from the object/yourself):

     Before: _____

     During: _____

     After: _____

Thoughts: (usually from you)

     Before: _____

     During: _____

     After: _____

Words/Statements (from the object/yourself):

     Before: _____

     During: _____

     After: _____

Attributes & characteristics experience: _____

_____

Surface/Texture: _____

Composition: _____

Temperature: _____

Density: _____

Movement: _____

Location/place: _____

Live Plant Object Challenge 3:

Select a live plant object that is not ethereal. Diagram the object in the space below. Connect and engage with the object through the Divine-Self aspect using the information and techniques from the workbook and workshop. Record information pertaining to that experience.

Diagram the object in the Walking Meditations' path containing the object

Date:_____ Start Time:_____ End Time:_____

Sound(s) used: _____

Aroma(s) used: _____

POI targeted:

    Hands:_____

    Feet: _____

Expectations: _____

_____

Sensory information (usually from object):

     Before: _____

     During: _____

     After: _____

Emotions/Feelings (from the object/yourself):

     Before: _____

     During: _____

     After: _____

Thoughts: (usually from you)

     Before: _____

     During: _____

     After: _____

Words/Statements (from the object/yourself):

     Before: _____

     During: _____

     After: _____

Attributes & characteristics experience: _____

_____

Surface/Texture: _____

Composition: _____

Temperature: _____

Density: _____

Movement: _____

Location/place: _____

Live Tree Object Challenge 1:

Select a live tree object that is not ethereal. Diagram the object in the space below. Connect and engage with the object through the Divine-Self aspect using the information and techniques from the workbook and workshop. Record information pertaining to that experience.

Diagram the object in the Walking Meditations' path containing the object

Date:_____ Start Time:_____ End Time:_____

Sound(s) used: _____

Aroma(s) used: _____

POI targeted:

      Hands:_____

      Feet: _____

Expectations: _____

_____

Sensory information (usually from object):

    Before: _____

    During: _____

    After: _____

Emotions/Feelings (from the object/yourself):

    Before: _____

    During: _____

    After: _____

Thoughts: (usually from you)

    Before: _____

    During: _____

    After: _____

Words/Statements (from the object/yourself):

    Before: _____

    During: _____

    After: _____

Attributes & characteristics experience: _____

_____

Surface/Texture: _____

Composition: _____

Temperature: _____

Density: _____

Movement: _____

Location/place: _____

Live Tree Object Challenge 2:

Select a live tree object that is not ethereal. Diagram the object in the space below. Connect and engage with the object through the Divine-Self aspect using the information and techniques from the workbook and workshop. Record information pertaining to that experience.

Diagram the object in the Walking Meditations' path containing the object

---

Date:_____   Start Time:_____   End Time:_____

Sound(s) used: _____

Aroma(s) used: _____

POI targeted:

      Hands:_____

      Feet: _____

Expectations: _____

_____

Sensory information (usually from object):

    Before: _____

    During: _____

    After: _____

Emotions/Feelings (from the object/yourself):

    Before: _____

    During: _____

    After: _____

Thoughts: (usually from you)

    Before: _____

    During: _____

    After: _____

Words/Statements (from the object/yourself):

    Before: _____

    During: _____

    After: _____

Attributes & characteristics experience: _____

_____

Surface/Texture: _____

Composition: _____

Temperature: _____

Density: _____

Movement: _____

Location/place: _____

Live Tree Object Challenge 3:

Select a live tree object that is not ethereal. Diagram the object in the space below. Connect and engage with the object through the Divine-Self aspect using the information and techniques from the workbook and workshop. Record information pertaining to that experience.

Diagram the object in the Walking Meditations' path containing the object

Date:_____   Start Time:_____   End Time:_____

Sound(s) used: _____

Aroma(s) used: _____

POI targeted:

      Hands:_____

      Feet: _____

Expectations: _____

_____

Sensory information (usually from object):

    Before: _____

    During: _____

    After: _____

Emotions/Feelings (from the object/yourself):

    Before: _____

    During: _____

    After: _____

Thoughts: (usually from you)

    Before: _____

    During: _____

    After: _____

Words/Statements (from the object/yourself):

    Before: _____

    During: _____

    After: _____

Attributes & characteristics experience: _____

_____

Surface/Texture: _____

Composition: _____

Temperature: _____

Density: _____

Movement: _____

Location/place: _____

Vegetable Object Challenge 1:

Select a vegetable object that is not ethereal. Diagram the object in the space below. Connect and engage with the object through the Divine-Self aspect using the information and techniques from the workbook and workshop. Record information pertaining to that experience.

Diagram the object in the Walking Meditations' path containing the object

Date:_____   Start Time:_____   End Time:_____

Sound(s) used: _____

Aroma(s) used: _____

POI targeted:

       Hands:_____

       Feet: _____

Expectations: _____

_____

Sensory information (usually from object):

    Before: _____

    During: _____

    After: _____

Emotions/Feelings (from the object/yourself):

    Before: _____

    During: _____

    After: _____

Thoughts: (usually from you)

    Before: _____

    During: _____

    After: _____

Words/Statements (from the object/yourself):

    Before: _____

    During: _____

    After: _____

Attributes & characteristics experience: _____

_____

Surface/Texture: _____

Composition: _____

Temperature: _____

Density: _____

Movement: _____

Location/place: _____

Vegetable Object Challenge 2:

Select a vegetable object that is not ethereal. Diagram the object in the space below. Connect and engage with the object through the Divine-Self aspect using the information and techniques from the workbook and workshop. Record information pertaining to that experience.

Diagram the object in the Walking Meditations' path containing the object

---

Date:_____   Start Time:_____   End Time:_____

Sound(s) used: _____

Aroma(s) used: _____

POI targeted:

      Hands:_____

      Feet: _____

Expectations: _____

_____

Sensory information (usually from object):

     Before: _____

     During: _____

     After: _____

Emotions/Feelings (from the object/yourself):

     Before: _____

     During: _____

     After: _____

Thoughts: (usually from you)

     Before: _____

     During: _____

     After: _____

Words/Statements (from the object/yourself):

     Before: _____

     During: _____

     After: _____

Attributes & characteristics experience: _____

_____

Surface/Texture: _____

Composition: _____

Temperature: _____

Density: _____

Movement: _____

Location/place: _____

Vegetable Object Challenge 3:

Select a vegetable object that is not ethereal. Diagram the object in the space below. Connect and engage with the object through the Divine-Self aspect using the information and techniques from the workbook and workshop. Record information pertaining to that experience.

Diagram the object in the Walking Meditations' path containing the object

---

Date:_____ Start Time:_____ End Time:_____

Sound(s) used: _____

Aroma(s) used: _____

POI targeted:

      Hands:_____

      Feet: _____

Expectations: _____

_____

Sensory information (usually from object):

     Before: _____

     During: _____

     After: _____

Emotions/Feelings (from the object/yourself):

     Before: _____

     During: _____

     After: _____

Thoughts: (usually from you)

     Before: _____

     During: _____

     After: _____

Words/Statements (from the object/yourself):

     Before: _____

     During: _____

     After: _____

Attributes & characteristics experience: _____

_____

Surface/Texture: _____

Composition: _____

Temperature: _____

Density: _____

Movement: _____

Location/place: _____

Food Object Challenge 1:

Select a food object that is not a vegetable or ethereal. Diagram the object in the space below. Connect and engage with the object through the Divine-Self aspect using the information and techniques from the workbook and workshop. Record the experience.

Diagram the object in the Walking Meditations' path containing the object

Date:_____ Start Time:_____ End Time:_____

Sound(s) used: _____

Aroma(s) used: _____

POI targeted:

       Hands:_____

       Feet: _____

Expectations: _____

_____

Sensory information (usually from object):

    Before: _____

    During: _____

    After: _____

Emotions/Feelings (from the object/yourself):

    Before: _____

    During: _____

    After: _____

Thoughts: (usually from you)

    Before: _____

    During: _____

    After: _____

Words/Statements (from the object/yourself):

    Before: _____

    During: _____

    After: _____

Attributes & characteristics experience: _____

_____

Surface/Texture: _____

Composition: _____

Temperature: _____

Density: _____

Movement: _____

Location/place: _____

Food Object Challenge 2:

Select a food object that is not a vegetable or ethereal. Diagram the object in the space below. Connect and engage with the object through the Divine-Self aspect using the information and techniques from the workbook and workshop. Record the experience.

Diagram the object in the Walking Meditations' path containing the object

---

Date:_____   Start Time:_____   End Time:_____

Sound(s) used: _____

Aroma(s) used: _____

POI targeted:

      Hands:_____

      Feet: _____

Expectations: _____

_____

Sensory information (usually from object):

    Before: _____

    During: _____

    After: _____

Emotions/Feelings (from the object/yourself):

    Before: _____

    During: _____

    After: _____

Thoughts: (usually from you)

    Before: _____

    During: _____

    After: _____

Words/Statements (from the object/yourself):

    Before: _____

    During: _____

    After: _____

Attributes & characteristics experience: _____

_____

Surface/Texture: _____

Composition: _____

Temperature: _____

Density: _____

Movement: _____

Location/place: _____

Food Object Challenge 3:

Select a food object that is not a vegetable or ethereal. Diagram the object in the space below. Connect and engage with the object through the Divine-Self aspect using the information and techniques from the workbook and workshop. Record the experience.

```
Diagram the object in the Walking Meditations' path containing the object
```

Date:_____   Start Time:_____   End Time:_____

Sound(s) used: _____

Aroma(s) used: _____

POI targeted:

        Hands:_____

        Feet: _____

Expectations: _____

_____

Sensory information (usually from object):

    Before: _____

    During: _____

    After: _____

Emotions/Feelings (from the object/yourself):

    Before: _____

    During: _____

    After: _____

Thoughts: (usually from you)

    Before: _____

    During: _____

    After: _____

Words/Statements (from the object/yourself):

    Before: _____

    During: _____

    After: _____

Attributes & characteristics experience: _____

_____

Surface/Texture: _____

Composition: _____

Temperature: _____

Density: _____

Movement: _____

Location/place: _____

Structure Object Challenge 1:

Select a structure object that is not ethereal. Diagram the object in the space below. Connect and engage with the object through the Divine-Self aspect using the information and techniques from the workbook and workshop. Record information pertaining to that experience.

Diagram the object in the Walking Meditations' path containing the object

Date:_____   Start Time:_____   End Time:_____

Sound(s) used: _____

Aroma(s) used: _____

POI targeted:

      Hands: _____

      Feet: _____

Expectations: _____

_____

Sensory information (usually from object):

    Before: _____

    During: _____

    After: _____

Emotions/Feelings (from the object/yourself):

    Before: _____

    During: _____

    After: _____

Thoughts: (usually from you)

    Before: _____

    During: _____

    After: _____

Words/Statements (from the object/yourself):

    Before: _____

    During: _____

    After: _____

Attributes & characteristics experience: _____

_____

Surface/structure: _____

Composition: _____

Temperature: _____

Movement: _____

Contents: _____

Location/place: _____

Surroundings: _____

Structure Object Challenge 2:

Select a structure object that is not ethereal. Diagram the object in the space below. Connect and engage with the object through the Divine-Self aspect using the information and techniques from the workbook and workshop. Record information pertaining to that experience.

Diagram the object in the Walking Meditations' path containing the object

Date:_____   Start Time:_____   End Time:_____

Sound(s) used: _____

Aroma(s) used: _____

POI targeted:

          Hands: _____

          Feet: _____

Expectations: _____

_____

Sensory information (usually from object):

    Before: _____

    During: _____

    After: _____

Emotions/Feelings (from the object/yourself):

    Before: _____

    During: _____

    After: _____

Thoughts: (usually from you)

    Before: _____

    During: _____

    After: _____

Words/Statements (from the object/yourself):

    Before: _____

    During: _____

    After: _____

Attributes & characteristics experience: _____

_____

Surface/structure: _____

Composition: _____

Temperature: _____

Movement: _____

Contents: _____

Location/place: _____

Surroundings: _____

Structure Object Challenge 3:

Select a structure object that is not ethereal. Diagram the object in the space below. Connect and engage with the object through the Divine-Self aspect using the information and techniques from the workbook and workshop. Record information pertaining to that experience.

Diagram the object in the Walking Meditations' path containing the object

Date:_____ Start Time:_____ End Time:_____

Sound(s) used: _____

Aroma(s) used: _____

POI targeted:

      Hands: _____

      Feet: _____

Expectations: _____

_____

Sensory information (usually from object):

    Before: _____

    During: _____

    After: _____

Emotions/Feelings (from the object/yourself):

    Before: _____

    During: _____

    After: _____

Thoughts: (usually from you)

    Before: _____

    During: _____

    After: _____

Words/Statements (from the object/yourself):

    Before: _____

    During: _____

    After: _____

Attributes & characteristics experience: _____

_____

Surface/structure: _____

Composition: _____

Temperature: _____

Movement: _____

Contents: _____

Location/place: _____

Surroundings: _____

Street Area Object Challenge 1*:

Select the street that you live on. Diagram the object in the space below. Connect and engage with the object through the Divine-Self aspect using the information and techniques from the workbook and workshop. Record the experience. *Complete the structure challenge before doing this one.

Diagram the object in the Walking Meditations' path containing the object

Date:_____   Start Time:_____   End Time:_____

Sound(s) used: _____

Aroma(s) used: _____

POI targeted:

      Hands:_____

      Feet: _____

Expectations: _____

_____

Sensory information (usually from object):

    Before: _____

    During: _____

    After: _____

Emotions/Feelings (from the object/yourself):

    Before: _____

    During: _____

    After: _____

Thoughts: (usually from you)

    Before: _____

    During: _____

    After: _____

Words/Statements (from the object/yourself):

    Before: _____

    During: _____

    After: _____

Attributes & characteristics experience: _____

_____

Size: _____

Layout: _____

Contents: _____

Temperature: _____

Movement: _____

Location: _____

Surroundings: _____

Street Area Object Challenge 2*:

Select the street that you live on. Diagram the object in the space below. Connect and engage with the object through the Divine-Self aspect using the information and techniques from the workbook and workshop. Record the experience. *Complete the structure challenge before doing this one.

Diagram the object in the Walking Meditations' path containing the object

Date:_____ Start Time:_____ End Time:_____

Sound(s) used: _____

Aroma(s) used: _____

POI targeted:

       Hands:_____

       Feet: _____

Expectations: _____

_____

Sensory information (usually from object):

    Before: _____

    During: _____

    After: _____

Emotions/Feelings (from the object/yourself):

    Before: _____

    During: _____

    After: _____

Thoughts: (usually from you)

    Before: _____

    During: _____

    After: _____

Words/Statements (from the object/yourself):

    Before: _____

    During: _____

    After: _____

Attributes & characteristics experience: _____

_____

Size: _____

Layout: _____

Contents: _____

Temperature: _____

Movement: _____

Location: _____

Surroundings: _____

Street Area Object Challenge 3*:

Select the street that you live on. Diagram the object in the space below. Connect and engage with the object through the Divine-Self aspect using the information and techniques from the workbook and workshop. Record the experience. *Complete the structure challenge before doing this one.

Diagram the object in the Walking Meditations' path containing the object

Date:_____   Start Time:_____   End Time:_____

Sound(s) used: _____

Aroma(s) used: _____

POI targeted:

      Hands:_____

      Feet: _____

Expectations: _____

_____

Sensory information (usually from object):

     Before: _____

     During:_____

     After: _____

Emotions/Feelings (from the object/yourself):

     Before: _____

     During: _____

     After: _____

Thoughts: (usually from you)

     Before:_____

     During: _____

     After:_____

Words/Statements (from the object/yourself):

     Before: _____

     During: _____

     After: _____

Attributes & characteristics experience: _____

_____

Size: _____

Layout: _____

Contents: _____

Temperature: _____

Movement: _____

Location:_____

Surroundings: _____

Community Area Object Challenge 1*:

Select the community you live in. Diagram the object in the space below. Connect and engage with the object through the Divine-Self aspect using the information and techniques from the workbook and workshop. Record the experience. Complete the street challenge first.

Diagram the object in the Walking Meditations' path containing the object

---

Date:_____   Start Time:_____   End Time:_____

Sound(s) used: _____

Aroma(s) used: _____

POI targeted:

       Hands:_____

       Feet: _____

Expectations: _____

_____

_____

Sensory information (usually from object):

    Before: _____

    During:_____

    After: _____

Emotions/Feelings (from the object/yourself):

    Before: _____

    During: _____

    After: _____

Thoughts: (usually from you)

    Before:_____

    During: _____

    After:_____

Words/Statements (from the object/yourself):

    Before: _____

    During: _____

    After: _____

Attributes & characteristics experience: _____

_____

Size: _____

Layout: _____

Contents: _____

Temperature: _____

Movement: _____

Location:_____

Surroundings: _____

Community Area Object Challenge 2*:

Select the community you live in. Diagram the object in the space below. Connect and engage with the object through the Divine-Self aspect using the information and techniques from the workbook and workshop. Record the experience. Complete the street challenge first.

```
Diagram the object in the Walking Meditations' path containing the object
```

Date:_____   Start Time:_____   End Time:_____

Sound(s) used: _____

Aroma(s) used: _____

POI targeted:

      Hands:_____

      Feet: _____

Expectations: _____

_____

_____

Sensory information (usually from object):

      Before: _____

      During:_____

      After: _____

Emotions/Feelings (from the object/yourself):

      Before: _____

      During: _____

      After: _____

Thoughts: (usually from you)

      Before:_____

      During: _____

      After:_____

Words/Statements (from the object/yourself):

      Before: _____

      During: _____

      After: _____

Attributes & characteristics experience: _____

_____

Size: _____

Layout: _____

Contents: _____

Temperature: _____

Movement: _____

Location:_____

Surroundings: _____

Community Area Object Challenge 3*:

Select the community you live in. Diagram the object in the space below. Connect and engage with the object through the Divine-Self aspect using the information and techniques from the workbook and workshop. Record the experience. Complete the street challenge first.

Diagram the object in the Walking Meditations' path containing the object

---

Date:_____ Start Time:_____ End Time:_____

Sound(s) used: _____

Aroma(s) used: _____

POI targeted:

      Hands:_____

      Feet: _____

Expectations: _____

_____

_____

Sensory information (usually from object):

     Before: _____

     During:_____

     After: _____

Emotions/Feelings (from the object/yourself):

     Before: _____

     During: _____

     After: _____

Thoughts: (usually from you)

     Before:_____

     During: _____

     After:_____

Words/Statements (from the object/yourself):

     Before: _____

     During: _____

     After: _____

Attributes & characteristics experience: _____

_____

Size: _____

Layout: _____

Contents: _____

Temperature: _____

Movement: _____

Location:_____

Surroundings: _____

City/Township Area Object Challenge 1*:

Select the city or township you live in. Diagram the object in the space below. Connect and engage with the object through the Divine-Self aspect using the information and techniques from the workbook and workshop. Record the experience. Complete the community challenge.

Diagram the object in the Walking Meditations' path containing the object

Date:_____ Start Time:_____ End Time:_____

Sound(s) used: _____

Aroma(s) used: _____

POI targeted:

Hands:_____

Feet: _____

Expectations: _____

_____

_____

Sensory information (usually from object):

    Before: _____

    During:_____

    After: _____

Emotions/Feelings (from the object/yourself):

    Before: _____

    During: _____

    After: _____

Thoughts: (usually from you)

    Before:_____

    During: _____

    After:_____

Words/Statements (from the object/yourself):

    Before: _____

    During: _____

    After: _____

Attributes & characteristics experience: _____

_____

Size: _____

Layout: _____

Contents: _____

Temperature: _____

Movement: _____

Location:_____

Surroundings: _____

City/Township Area Object Challenge 2*:

Select the city or township you live in. Diagram the object in the space below. Connect and engage with the object through the Divine-Self aspect using the information and techniques from the workbook and workshop. Record the experience. Complete the community challenge.

> Diagram the object in the Walking Meditations' path containing the object

Date:_____   Start Time:_____   End Time:_____

Sound(s) used: _____

Aroma(s) used: _____

POI targeted:

      Hands:_____

      Feet: _____

Expectations: _____

_____

_____

Sensory information (usually from object):

    Before: _____

    During:_____

    After: _____

Emotions/Feelings (from the object/yourself):

    Before: _____

    During: _____

    After: _____

Thoughts: (usually from you)

    Before:_____

    During: _____

    After:_____

Words/Statements (from the object/yourself):

    Before: _____

    During: _____

    After: _____

Attributes & characteristics experience: _____

_____

Size: _____

Layout: _____

Contents: _____

Temperature: _____

Movement: _____

Location:_____

Surroundings: _____

City/Township Area Object Challenge 3*:

Select the city or township you live in. Diagram the object in the space below. Connect and engage with the object through the Divine-Self aspect using the information and techniques from the workbook and workshop. Record the experience. Complete the community challenge.

Diagram the object in the Walking Meditations' path containing the object

Date:_____   Start Time:_____   End Time:_____

Sound(s) used: _____

Aroma(s) used: _____

POI targeted:

      Hands:_____

      Feet: _____

Expectations: _____

_____

_____

Sensory information (usually from object):

    Before: _____

    During:_____

    After: _____

Emotions/Feelings (from the object/yourself):

    Before: _____

    During: _____

    After: _____

Thoughts: (usually from you)

    Before:_____

    During: _____

    After:_____

Words/Statements (from the object/yourself):

    Before: _____

    During: _____

    After: _____

Attributes & characteristics experience: _____

_____

Size: _____

Layout: _____

Contents: _____

Temperature: _____

Movement: _____

Location:_____

Surroundings: _____

Place Object Challenge 1*:

Select a place on the planet (land or ocean). Diagram the object in the space below. Connect and engage with the object through the Divine-Self aspect using the information and techniques from the workbook and workshop. Record the experience. Complete the city/township challenge first.

```
┌─────────────────────────────────────────────────────────┐
│ Diagram the object in the Walking Meditations' path       │
│ containing the object                                     │
│                                                           │
│                                                           │
│                                                           │
│                                                           │
│                                                           │
│                                                           │
│                                                           │
│                                                           │
└─────────────────────────────────────────────────────────┘
```

Date:_____   Start Time:_____   End Time:_____

Sound(s) used: _____

Aroma(s) used: _____

POI targeted:

        Hands:_____

        Feet: _____

Expectations: _____

_____

_____

Sensory information (usually from object):

      Before: _____

      During:_____

      After: _____

Emotions/Feelings (from the object/yourself):

      Before: _____

      During: _____

      After: _____

Thoughts: (usually from you)

      Before:_____

      During: _____

      After:_____

Words/Statements (from the object/yourself):

      Before: _____

      During: _____

      After: _____

Attributes & characteristics experience: _____

_____

Size: _____

Layout: _____

Contents: _____

Temperature: _____

Movement: _____

Location:_____

Surroundings: _____

Place Object Challenge 2*:

Select a place on the planet (land or ocean). Diagram the object in the space below. Connect and engage with the object through the Divine-Self aspect using the information and techniques from the workbook and workshop. Record the experience. Complete the city/township challenge first.

Diagram the object in the Walking Meditations' path containing the object

---

Date:_____ Start Time:_____ End Time:_____

Sound(s) used: _____

Aroma(s) used: _____

POI targeted:

      Hands:_____

      Feet: _____

Expectations: _____

_____

_____

Sensory information (usually from object):

    Before: _____

    During:_____

    After: _____

Emotions/Feelings (from the object/yourself):

    Before: _____

    During: _____

    After: _____

Thoughts: (usually from you)

    Before:_____

    During: _____

    After:_____

Words/Statements (from the object/yourself):

    Before: _____

    During: _____

    After: _____

Attributes & characteristics experience: _____

_____

Size: _____

Layout: _____

Contents: _____

Temperature: _____

Movement: _____

Location:_____

Surroundings: _____

Place Object Challenge 3*:

Select a place on the planet (land or ocean). Diagram the object in the space below. Connect and engage with the object through the Divine-Self aspect using the information and techniques from the workbook and workshop. Record the experience. Complete the city/township challenge first.

Diagram the object in the Walking Meditations' path containing the object

---

Date:_____   Start Time:_____   End Time:_____

Sound(s) used: _____

Aroma(s) used: _____

POI targeted:

      Hands:_____

      Feet: _____

Expectations: _____

_____

_____

Sensory information (usually from object):

      Before: _____

      During:_____

      After: _____

Emotions/Feelings (from the object/yourself):

      Before: _____

      During: _____

      After: _____

Thoughts: (usually from you)

      Before:_____

      During: _____

      After:_____

Words/Statements (from the object/yourself):

      Before: _____

      During: _____

      After: _____

Attributes & characteristics experience: _____

_____

Size: _____

Layout: _____

Contents: _____

Temperature: _____

Movement: _____

Location:_____

Surroundings: _____

Organ Object Challenge 1:

Select an organ in your body. Diagram the object in the space below. The goal is to become familiar with the organ in order to detect an abnormality if it arises. Connect and engage with the object through the Divine-Self aspect using the information and techniques from the workbook and workshop. Record the experience.

Diagram the object in the Walking Meditations' path containing the object

Date:_____ Start Time:_____ End Time:_____

Sound(s) used: _____

Aroma(s) used: _____

POI targeted:

      Hands:_____

      Feet: _____

Expectations: _____

_____

_____

Sensory information (usually from object):

Before: _____

During: _____

After: _____

Emotions/Feelings (from the object/yourself):

Before:_____

During: _____

After: _____

Thoughts: (usually from you)

Before: _____

During: _____

After: _____

Words/Statements (from the object/yourself):

Before: _____

During: _____

After: _____

Attributes & characteristics experience: _____

Size/shape: _____

Density/Structural mass: _____

Temperature: _____

Rhythmic sensations: _____

Location: _____

Contents: _____

Surroundings: _____

Connections: _____

Feeling:

Relaxed ____Tense ____Excited ____Strained ____Other _____

144

Organ Object Challenge 2:

Select an organ in your body. Diagram the object in the space below. The goal is to become familiar with the organ in order to detect an abnormality if it arises. Connect and engage with the object through the Divine-Self aspect using the information and techniques from the workbook and workshop. Record the experience.

Diagram the object in the Walking Meditations' path containing the object

---

Date:_____   Start Time:_____   End Time:_____

Sound(s) used: _____

Aroma(s) used: _____

POI targeted:

      Hands:_____

      Feet: _____

Expectations: _____

_____

_____

Sensory information (usually from object):

    Before: _____

    During: _____

    After: _____

Emotions/Feelings (from the object/yourself):

    Before:_____

    During: _____

    After: _____

Thoughts: (usually from you)

    Before: _____

    During: _____

    After: _____

Words/Statements (from the object/yourself):

    Before: _____

    During: _____

    After: _____

Attributes & characteristics experience: _____

Size/shape: _____

Density/Structural mass: _____

Temperature: _____

Rhythmic sensations: _____

Location: _____

Contents: _____

Surroundings: _____

Connections: _____

Feeling:

Relaxed ____Tense ____Excited ____Strained ____Other _____

Organ Object Challenge 3:

Select an organ in your body. Diagram the object in the space below. The goal is to become familiar with the organ in order to detect an abnormality if it arises. Connect and engage with the object through the Divine-Self aspect using the information and techniques from the workbook and workshop. Record the experience.

Diagram the object in the Walking Meditations' path containing the object

---

Date:_____   Start Time:_____   End Time:_____

Sound(s) used: _____

Aroma(s) used: _____

POI targeted:

     Hands:_____

     Feet: _____

Expectations: _____

_____

Sensory information (usually from object):

　　　Before: _____

　　　During: _____

　　　After: _____

Emotions/Feelings (from the object/yourself):

　　　Before:_____

　　　During: _____

　　　After: _____

Thoughts: (usually from you)

　　　Before: _____

　　　During: _____

　　　After: _____

Words/Statements (from the object/yourself):

　　　Before: _____

　　　During: _____

　　　After: _____

Attributes & characteristics experience: _____

 Size/shape: _____

Density/Structural mass: _____

Temperature: _____

Rhythmic sensations: _____

Location: _____

Contents: _____

Surroundings: _____

Connections: _____

Feeling:

Relaxed ____Tense ____Excited ____Strained ____Other _____

Body Part Object Challenge 1*:

Select a body part on your body. Diagram the object in the space below. The goal is to become familiar with the body part in order to detect an abnormality if it arises. Connect and engage with the object through the Divine-Self aspect using the information and techniques from the workbook and workshop. Record the experience. *Complete the organ challenge before doing this one.

Diagram the object in the Walking Meditations' path containing the object

---

Date:_____   Start Time:_____   End Time:_____

Sound(s) used: _____

Aroma(s) used: _____

POI targeted:

       Hands:_____

       Feet: _____

Expectations: _____

_____

Sensory information (usually from object):

    Before: _____

    During: _____

    After: _____

Emotions/Feelings (from the object/yourself):

    Before:_____

    During: _____

    After: _____

Thoughts: (usually from you)

    Before: _____

    During: _____

    After: _____

Words/Statements (from the object/yourself):

    Before: _____

    During: _____

    After: _____

Attributes & characteristics experience: _____

Size/shape: _____

Density/Structural mass: _____

Temperature: _____

Rhythmic sensations: _____

Location: _____

Contents: _____

Surroundings: _____

Connections: _____

Feeling:

Relaxed ____Tense ____Excited ____Strained ____Other _____

Body Part Object Challenge 2*:

Select a body part on your body. Diagram the object in the space below. The goal is to become familiar with the body part in order to detect an abnormality if it arises. Connect and engage with the object through the Divine-Self aspect using the information and techniques from the workbook and workshop. Record the experience. *Complete the organ challenge before doing this one.

Diagram the object in the Walking Meditations' path containing the object

Date:_____   Start Time:_____   End Time:_____

Sound(s) used: _____

Aroma(s) used: _____

POI targeted:

      Hands:_____

      Feet: _____

Expectations: _____

Sensory information (usually from object):

    Before: _____

    During: _____

    After: _____

Emotions/Feelings (from the object/yourself):

    Before:_____

    During: _____

    After: _____

Thoughts: (usually from you)

    Before: _____

    During: _____

    After: _____

Words/Statements (from the object/yourself):

    Before: _____

    During: _____

    After: _____

Attributes & characteristics experience: _____

Size/shape: _____

Density/Structural mass: _____

Temperature: _____

Rhythmic sensations: _____

Location: _____

Contents: _____

Surroundings: _____

Connections: _____

Feeling:

Relaxed ____Tense ____Excited ____Strained ____Other _____

Body Part Object Challenge 3*:

Select a body part on your body. Diagram the object in the space below. The goal is to become familiar with the body part in order to detect an abnormality if it arises. Connect and engage with the object through the Divine-Self aspect using the information and techniques from the workbook and workshop. Record the experience. *Complete the organ challenge before doing this one.

Diagram the object in the Walking Meditations' path containing the object

---

Date:_____   Start Time:_____   End Time:_____

Sound(s) used: _____

Aroma(s) used: _____

POI targeted:

      Hands:_____

      Feet: _____

Expectations: _____

Sensory information (usually from object):

     Before: _____

     During: _____

     After: _____

Emotions/Feelings (from the object/yourself):

     Before:_____

     During: _____

     After: _____

Thoughts: (usually from you)

     Before: _____

     During: _____

     After: _____

Words/Statements (from the object/yourself):

     Before: _____

     During: _____

     After: _____

Attributes & characteristics experience: _____

Size/shape: _____

Density/Structural mass: _____

Temperature: _____

Rhythmic sensations: _____

Location: _____

Contents: _____

Surroundings: _____

Connections: _____

Feeling:

Relaxed ____Tense ____Excited ____Strained ____Other _____

People Object Challenge 1:

Select a person. Diagram the person in the space below. The goal is to become familiar with the person (similar to walking in his/her shoes). Connect and engage with the person through the Divine-Self aspect using the information and techniques from the workbook and workshop. Record the experience. Personal information and external characteristics should not be involved.

Diagram the object in the Walking Meditations' path containing the object

Date:_____ Start Time:_____ End Time:_____

Sound(s) used: _____

Aroma(s) used: _____

POI targeted:

     Hands:_____

     Feet: _____

Expectations: _____

Sensory information (usually from object):

    Before: _____

    During: _____

    After: _____

Emotions/Feelings (from the object/yourself):

    Before: _____

    During: _____

    After: _____

Thoughts: (usually from you)

    Before: _____

    During: _____

    After: _____

Words/Statements (from the object/yourself):

    Before: _____

    During: _____

    After: _____

The concerned here is the characteristic and what produces it:

Emotions: _____

Mood/Temperament: _____

Behavior: _____

Energy level/type: _____

Thought:_____

Process:_____

Personality: _____

Surroundings: _____

Learning type/method: _____

Idiosyncrasies: _____

People Object Challenge 2:

Select a person. Diagram the person in the space below. The goal is to become familiar with the person (similar to walking in his/her shoes). Connect and engage with the person through the Divine-Self aspect using the information and techniques from the workbook and workshop. Record the experience. Personal information and external characteristics should not be involved.

Diagram the object in the Walking Meditations' path containing the object

Date:_____   Start Time:_____   End Time:_____

Sound(s) used: _____

Aroma(s) used: _____

POI targeted:

     Hands:_____

     Feet: _____

Expectations: _____

_____

Sensory information (usually from object):

    Before: _____

    During: _____

    After: _____

Emotions/Feelings (from the object/yourself):

    Before: _____

    During: _____

    After: _____

Thoughts: (usually from you)

    Before: _____

    During: _____

    After: _____

Words/Statements (from the object/yourself):

    Before: _____

    During: _____

    After: _____

The concerned here is the characteristic and what produces it:

Emotions: _____

Mood/Temperament: _____

Behavior: _____

Energy level/type: _____

Thought:_____

Process:_____

Personality: _____

Surroundings: _____

Learning type/method: _____

Idiosyncrasies: _____

People Object Challenge 3:

Select a person. Diagram the person in the space below. The goal is to become familiar with the person (similar to walking in his/her shoes). Connect and engage with the person through the Divine-Self aspect using the information and techniques from the workbook and workshop. Record the experience. Personal information and external characteristics should not be involved.

Diagram the object in the Walking Meditations' path containing the object

Date:_____   Start Time:_____   End Time:_____

Sound(s) used: _____

Aroma(s) used: _____

POI targeted:

      Hands:_____

      Feet: _____

Expectations: _____

_____

Sensory information (usually from object):

    Before: _____

    During: _____

    After: _____

Emotions/Feelings (from the object/yourself):

    Before: _____

    During: _____

    After: _____

Thoughts: (usually from you)

    Before: _____

    During: _____

    After: _____

Words/Statements (from the object/yourself):

    Before: _____

    During: _____

    After: _____

The concerned here is the characteristic and what produces it:

Emotions: _____

Mood/Temperament: _____

Behavior: _____

Energy level/type: _____

Thought:_____

Process:_____

Personality: _____

Surroundings: _____

Learning type/method: _____

Idiosyncrasies: _____

Animal/Mammal Object Challenge 1:

Select an animal or mammal. Diagram the object in the space below. The goal is to become familiar with the animal or mammal. Connect and engage with it through the Divine-Self aspect using the information and techniques from the workbook and workshop. Record information pertaining to that experience.

Diagram the object in the Walking Meditations' path containing the object

Date:_____   Start Time:_____   End Time:_____

Sound(s) used: _____

Aroma(s) used: _____

POI targeted:

     Hands:_____

     Feet: _____

Expectations: _____

_____

_____

Sensory information (usually from object):

     Before: _____

     During: _____

     After: _____

Emotions/Feelings (from the object/yourself):

     Before: _____

     During: _____

     After: _____

Thoughts: (usually from you)

     Before: _____

     During: _____

     After: _____

Words/Statements (from the object/yourself):

     Before: _____

     During: _____

     After: _____

The concerned here is with what produces these characteristics:

Emotions: _____

Mood/Temperament: _____

Behavior: _____

Energy level/type: _____

Thought: _____

Process:_____

Personality: _____

Surroundings: _____

Learning type/method: _____

Peculiarities: _____

Animal/Mammal Object Challenge 2:

Select an animal or mammal. Diagram the object in the space below. The goal is to become familiar with the animal or mammal. Connect and engage with it through the Divine-Self aspect using the information and techniques from the workbook and workshop. Record information pertaining to that experience.

```
Diagram the object in the Walking Meditations' path containing the object
```

Date:_____ Start Time:_____ End Time:_____

Sound(s) used: _____

Aroma(s) used: _____

POI targeted:

      Hands:_____

      Feet: _____

Expectations: _____

_____

_____

Sensory information (usually from object):

    Before: _____

    During: _____

    After: _____

Emotions/Feelings (from the object/yourself):

    Before: _____

    During: _____

    After: _____

Thoughts: (usually from you)

    Before: _____

    During: _____

    After: _____

Words/Statements (from the object/yourself):

    Before: _____

    During: _____

    After: _____

The concerned here is with what produces these characteristics:

Emotions: _____

Mood/Temperament: _____

Behavior: _____

Energy level/type: _____

Thought: _____

Process:_____

Personality: _____

Surroundings: _____

Learning type/method: _____

Peculiarities: _____

Animal/Mammal Object Challenge 3:

Select an animal or mammal. Diagram the object in the space below. The goal is to become familiar with the animal or mammal. Connect and engage with it through the Divine-Self aspect using the information and techniques from the workbook and workshop. Record information pertaining to that experience.

Diagram the object in the Walking Meditations' path containing the object

Date:_____ Start Time:_____ End Time:_____

Sound(s) used: _____

Aroma(s) used: _____

POI targeted:

Hands:_____

Feet: _____

Expectations: _____

_____

_____

Sensory information (usually from object):

    Before: _____

    During: _____

    After: _____

Emotions/Feelings (from the object/yourself):

    Before: _____

    During: _____

    After: _____

Thoughts: (usually from you)

    Before: _____

    During: _____

    After: _____

Words/Statements (from the object/yourself):

    Before: _____

    During: _____

    After: _____

The concerned here is with what produces these characteristics:

Emotions: _____

Mood/Temperament: _____

Behavior: _____

Energy level/type: _____

Thought: _____

Process:_____

Personality: _____

Surroundings: _____

Learning type/method: _____

Peculiarities: _____

Part 3

Walking Meditations

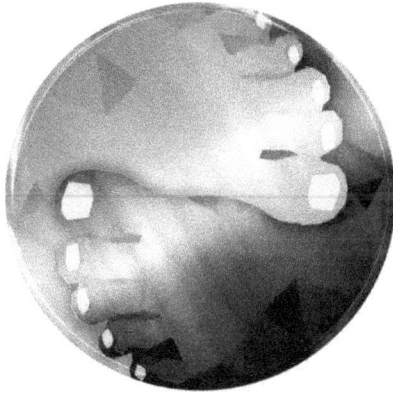

Your world is the results of your meditations

Walking Meditations 1:

Use the techniques learned in the workshop and the steps in the Walking Meditations workbook to create paths and altars. Practice engaging with objects and record your information below.

Date:_____   Time:_____am/pm

Objects: _____

_____

_____

_____

_____

_____

Walking Meditations 2:

Use the techniques learned in the workshop and the steps in the Walking Meditations workbook to create paths and altars. Practice engaging with objects and record your information below.

Date:_____   Time:_____am/pm

Objects: _____

_____

_____

_____

_____

_____

Walking Meditations 3:

Use the techniques learned in the workshop and the steps in the Walking Meditations workbook to create paths and altars. Practice engaging with objects and record your information below.

Date:_____   Time:_____am/pm

Objects: _____

_____

_____

_____

_____

_____

Walking Meditations 4:

Use the techniques learned in the workshop and the steps in the Walking Meditations workbook to create paths and altars. Practice engaging with objects and record your information below.

Date:_____   Time:_____am/pm

Objects: _____

_____

_____

_____

_____

_____

Walking Meditations 5:

Use the techniques learned in the workshop and the steps in the Walking Meditations workbook to create paths and altars. Practice engaging with objects and record your information below.

Date:_____   Time:_____am/pm

Objects: _____

_____

_____

_____

_____

_____

Walking Meditations 6:

Use the techniques learned in the workshop and the steps in the Walking Meditations workbook to create paths and altars. Practice engaging with objects and record your information below.

Date:_____   Time:_____am/pm

Objects: _____

_____

_____

_____

_____

_____

Walking Meditations 7:

Use the techniques learned in the workshop and the steps in the Walking Meditations workbook to create paths and altars. Practice engaging with objects and record your information below.

Date:_____   Time:_____am/pm

Objects: _____

_____

_____

_____

_____

_____

Part 4

Manifesting

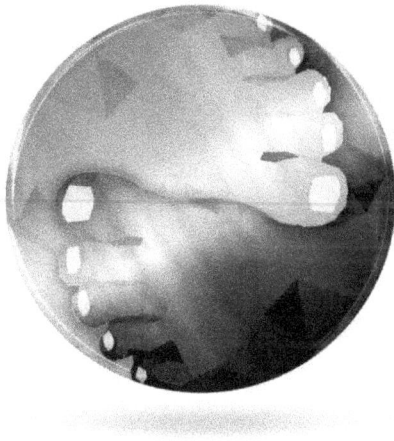

Meditation is the key to manifesting

Manifesting Challenge 1:

Select an easy object to manifest that does not involve another person. Use the techniques learned in the workshop and the steps in the Walking Meditations workbook pertaining to manifesting to complete this challenge. Your goal is bring a desired object into your daily life and into this physical realm. It may be helpful to create a path with an altar. Record information pertaining to that experience.

Sketch or picture of object on the Walking Meditations' path

Start date:_____ Actualized date:_____

Sound(s) used: _____

Aroma(s) used: _____

POI targeted:

      Hands/Feet: _____

Type of massage:

      Fingers ____ Thumbs ____ Combination ____

Length of massage used per hand:

185

Activation strokes used:

Tapping ____ Pressing ____ Circular ____ Combination ____

Expectations: _____

_____

Statements: _____

_____

Emotions/Feelings: _____

_____

Thoughts: _____

_____

Date object was integrated into the physical realm: _____

Quality of relationship:

needs improving _____ weak _____ strong _____

How was object integrated into your physical life? _____

_____

State your daily interactions with object: _____

_____

Pictures or other items used to manifest object: _____

_____

_____

_____

_____

_____

_____

Manifesting Challenge 2:

Select an easy object to manifest that does not involve another person. Use the techniques learned in the workshop and the steps in the Walking Meditations workbook pertaining to manifesting to complete this challenge. Your goal is bring a desired object into your daily life and into this physical realm. It may be helpful to create a path with an altar. Record information pertaining to that experience.

```
┌─────────────────────────────────────────────────────────┐
│ Sketch or picture of object on the Walking Meditations' path │
│                                                         │
│                                                         │
│                                                         │
│                                                         │
│                                                         │
│                                                         │
│                                                         │
│                                                         │
└─────────────────────────────────────────────────────────┘
```

Start date:_____ Actualized date:_____

Sound(s) used: _____

Aroma(s) used: _____

POI targeted:

      Hands/Feet: _____

Type of massage:

      Fingers ____ Thumbs ____ Combination ____

Length of massage used per hand:

187

Activation strokes used:

     Tapping ____ Pressing ____ Circular ____ Combination ____

Expectations: _____

_____

Statements: _____

_____

Emotions/Feelings: _____

_____

Thoughts: _____

_____

Date object was integrated into the physical realm: _____

Quality of relationship:

 needs improving _____ weak _____ strong _____

How was object integrated into your physical life? _____

_____

State your daily interactions with object: _____

_____

Pictures or other items used to manifest object: _____

_____

_____

_____

_____

_____

_____

Select an easy object to manifest that does not involve another person. Use the techniques learned in the workshop and the steps in the Walking Meditations workbook pertaining to manifesting to complete this challenge. Your goal is bring a desired object into your daily life and into this physical realm. It may be helpful to create a path with an altar. Record information pertaining to that experience.

Sketch or picture of object on the Walking Meditations' path

Start date:_____ Actualized date:_____

Sound(s) used: _____

Aroma(s) used: _____

POI targeted:

       Hands/Feet: _____

Type of massage:

       Fingers ____ Thumbs ____ Combination ____

Length of massage used per hand:

Activation strokes used:

      Tapping ____ Pressing ____ Circular ____ Combination ____

Expectations: _____

_____

Statements: _____

_____

Emotions/Feelings: _____

_____

Thoughts: _____

_____

Date object was integrated into the physical realm: _____

Quality of relationship:

 needs improving _____ weak _____ strong _____

How was object integrated into your physical life? _____

_____

State your daily interactions with object: _____

_____

Pictures or other items used to manifest object: _____

_____

_____

_____

_____

_____

_____

Manifesting Challenge 4:

Select an easy object to manifest that does not involve another person. Use the techniques learned in the workshop and the steps in the Walking Meditations workbook pertaining to manifesting to complete this challenge. Your goal is bring a desired object into your daily life and into this physical realm. It may be helpful to create a path with an altar. Record information pertaining to that experience.

```
Sketch or picture of object on the Walking Meditations' path



```

Start date:_____ Actualized date:_____

Sound(s) used: _____

Aroma(s) used: _____

POI targeted:

      Hands/Feet: _____

Type of massage:

      Fingers ____ Thumbs ____ Combination ____

Length of massage used per hand:

Activation strokes used:

      Tapping ___ Pressing ___ Circular ___ Combination ___

Expectations: _____

_____

Statements: _____

_____

Emotions/Feelings: _____

_____

Thoughts: _____

_____

Date object was integrated into the physical realm: _____

Quality of relationship:

 needs improving _____ weak _____ strong _____

How was object integrated into your physical life? _____

_____

State your daily interactions with object: _____

_____

Pictures or other items used to ma

nifest object: _____

_____

_____

_____

_____

_____

Manifesting Challenge 5:

Select an easy object to manifest that does not involve another person. Use the techniques learned in the workshop and the steps in the Walking Meditations workbook pertaining to manifesting to complete this challenge. Your goal is bring a desired object into your daily life and into this physical realm. It may be helpful to create a path with an altar. Record information pertaining to that experience.

```
Sketch or picture of object on the Walking Meditations' path




```

Start date:_____ Actualized date:_____

Sound(s) used: _____

Aroma(s) used: _____

POI targeted:

      Hands/Feet: _____

Type of massage:

      Fingers ____ Thumbs ____ Combination ____

Length of massage used per hand:

Activation strokes used:

Tapping ____ Pressing ____ Circular ____ Combination ____

Expectations: _____

_____

Statements: _____

_____

Emotions/Feelings: _____

_____

Thoughts: _____

_____

Date object was integrated into the physical realm: _____

Quality of relationship:

needs improving _____ weak _____ strong _____

How was object integrated into your physical life? _____

_____

State your daily interactions with object: _____

_____

Pictures or other items used to manifest object: _____

_____

_____

_____

_____

_____

_____

Manifesting Challenge 6:

Select an easy object to manifest that does not involve another person. Use the techniques learned in the workshop and the steps in the Walking Meditations workbook pertaining to manifesting to complete this challenge. Your goal is bring a desired object into your daily life and into this physical realm. It may be helpful to create a path with an altar. Record information pertaining to that experience.

```
┌─────────────────────────────────────────────────────────┐
│ Sketch or picture of object on the Walking Meditations' path │
│                                                         │
│                                                         │
│                                                         │
│                                                         │
│                                                         │
│                                                         │
│                                                         │
│                                                         │
│                                                         │
│                                                         │
└─────────────────────────────────────────────────────────┘
```

Start date:_____ Actualized date:_____

Sound(s) used: _____

Aroma(s) used: _____

POI targeted:

      Hands/Feet: _____

Type of massage:

      Fingers ___ Thumbs ___ Combination ___

Length of massage used per hand:

Activation strokes used:

Tapping ____ Pressing ____ Circular ____ Combination ____

Expectations: _____

_____

Statements: _____

_____

Emotions/Feelings: _____

_____

Thoughts: _____

_____

Date object was integrated into the physical realm: _____

Quality of relationship:

needs improving _____ weak _____ strong _____

How was object integrated into your physical life? _____

_____

State your daily interactions with object: _____

_____

Pictures or other items used to manifest object: _____

_____

_____

_____

_____

_____

_____

Part 5

Journaling

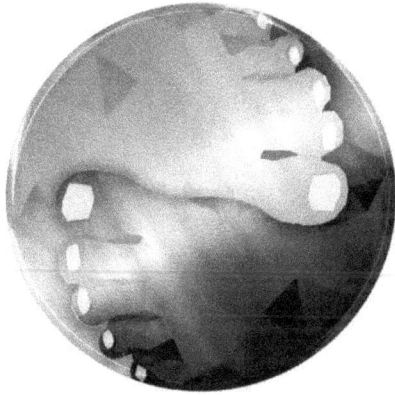

Meditation brings forth the most important information

Meditation helps you gain clarity

Your strength increases in the stillness you create during meditation

Achieve your desired goals through meditation

_____

_____

_____

_____

_____

_____

_____

_____

_____

_____

_____

_____

_____

_____

_____

_____

_____

_____

Use meditation to establish relationships that are more meaningful

True mastery begins with meditation

Meditation helps you access your hidden potential

Encounter the Divine nature of others through meditation

Use meditation to release the greatness within

Reshape your world through meditation

Use meditation to reach your desired state

Expand your awareness using meditation

The brightest light within you is reached through meditation

_____

_____

_____

_____

_____

_____

_____

_____

_____

_____

_____

_____

_____

_____

_____

_____

_____

_____

_____

Balance your inner and outer world through meditation

Polish and heighten your senses through meditation

Use meditation to pilot a course to success

Unleash your greatest potential through meditation

_____

_____

_____

_____

_____

_____

_____

_____

_____

_____

_____

_____

_____

_____

_____

_____

_____

_____

_____

_____

Move with greater levels of confidence using meditation

Stilling the flow of thoughts in your mind is the beginning of your greatness

Touching the Divine is made easy through meditation

Become more in-tuned with your surroundings and yourself using meditation

Meditation increases your focus and perception

A truer you is reached through meditation

Meditation brings clear sight

Vocabulary

Products

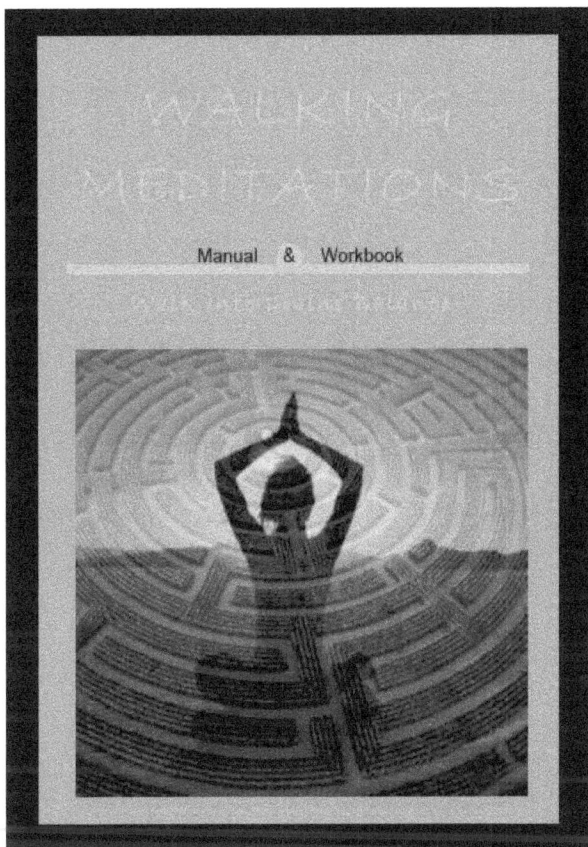

Walking Meditations Manual &Workbook
ISBN13: 978-1-62607-004-2
8.5" x 11" Perfectbound

Walking Meditations incorporates aspects of meditation, labyrinths, and sacred altars to help bring greater balance in your life. You gain a better understanding of yourself and the world around you using Walking Meditations. Easy techniques are intricately woven together to form a workable process of accessing and communicating with others. This powerful workbook combines non-traditional methods to help you develop the skills needed to journey through life with greater ease. The new toolset gained through Walking Meditations help you connect with and experience the world on a deeper level.

Essential Aroma Oil Blends

A little goes a long way and these blends are ready to be added to your favorite lotion, carrier oil, or diffuser. The aromatic blends range from a light floral to an exotic or earthy woody tone. These blends soothe and assist you in successfully bringing about a balanced state during Walking Meditations. Each beautiful blend consists of pure high grade uncut essential oils in a 1/8 oz bottle. Get your aromatic blends today by visiting www.walkingmeditations.org.

Floral Blends

F-CHAM11
A sweet floral blend containing a chamomile undertone soothes and relaxes.

F-LAV22
A sweet floral blend containing a lavender undertone soothes and de-stresses.

F-BOQ33
A special floral blend containing undertones soothes while heightening your senses.

Sacred Blends

S-FRK11
A refreshing woody blend containing a Frankincense undertone.

S-FM22
A refreshing exotic blend containing undertones of Frankincense and Myrrh.

S-HYS33
A strong refreshing blend containing undertones of Hyssop.

S-LTS44
A unique floral blend containing a Lotus blossom undertone.

S-MYR55
A smooth woody blend containing a Myrrh undertone.

S-NCHM66
A sweet exotic floral blend containing Nag Champa undertones.

S-PAT77
A strong woody blend containing a Patchouli undertone.

S-SAN88
A smooth woody blend containing a Sandalwood undertone.

S-YLG99
A woody and exotic floral blend containing Ylang-Ylang undertones.

MP3
Single recording, Digital download

*The mp3 recordings are designed to enhance your Walking Meditations'
experience. Use the specialized recordings to continue to practices during your
work with Walking Meditations to simulate your participation in a Walking
Meditations workshop. They can act as your personal instructions when setting
up Walking Meditations to making the important connection with Divine Self.
Order your copies today at www.walkingmeditations.org.*

Activating the Body

Approaching and Interacting with an Altar

**Approaching Walking Meditations and Interacting with the
path**

Awakening the Divine Self

Clair Essence Awareness

Constructing Altars (physical & ethereal)

Constructing physical & ethereal altars with Objects

Diagramming Walking Meditations (layout with altars)

Divine Self-Connections

Expand Your Divine Essence

Interacting with Aroma Blends in Walking Meditations

Interacting with Sounds during Walking Meditations

Preliminary Declarations

Moving Through Walking Meditations

Sensing the Divine Essence in Others

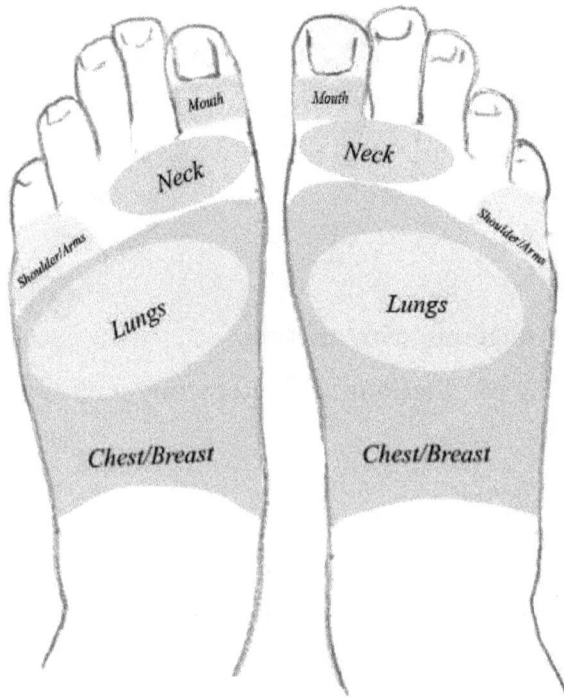

Left Foot   Right Foot

Mouth   Mouth

Neck   Neck

Shoulder/Arms   Shoulder/Arms

Lungs   Lungs

Chest/Breast   Chest/Breast

Color Reflexology Charts
Five-sheet laminated set

These are full color laminated pages displaying the POI (Points of Interest) of the hands and feet used in Walking Meditations. The charts are 8 ½" x 11" durable laminated pieces that allow you quickly reference the Points of Interest targeted in Walking Meditations. Visit www.walkingmeditations.org to get your set today.

Certified Walking Meditations Instructor

You can join our team and become a certified instructor of Walking Meditations. We are looking for individuals that enjoy working with others and have a desire to help others enhance and bring balance to their lives by using the tools they have learned then this may be a perfect fit for you. You will gain the skills to teach Walking Meditations techniques to others and conduct Walking Meditations workshops. Contact us through www.walkingmeditations.org for information regarding upcoming certification workshops.

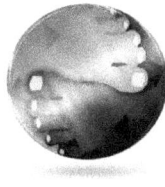

- Become certified to teach others the Walking Meditations techniques

- Help others enhance and balance their lives

- Learn to conduct Walking Meditations workshops

- Receive ongoing support

- Access to discounted products

- Wholesale discounts for Walking Meditations workbook

- Wholesale discounts for Walking Meditations Journal

- Wholesale discounts for Walking Meditations products

- Receive a certificate suitable for framing

- Laminated photo identification card

- List your workshop classes on the Walking Meditations website